The Great American Novel

by

William Carlos Williams

FOLCROFT LIBRARY EDITIONS / 1973

Library of Congress Cataloging in Publication Data

Williams, William Carlos, 1883-1963.
   The great American novel.

    I. Title.
PZ3.W67667Gr6 [PS3545.I544]   813'.5'2   73-2637
ISBN 0-8414-2809-3 (lib. bdg.)

The Great American Novel

by

William Carlos Williams

The Great
American Novel

CHAPTER I.

THE FOG.

IF THERE is progress then there is a novel. Without progress there is nothing. Everything exists from the beginning. I existed in the beginning. I was a slobbering infant. Today I saw nameless grasses—I tapped the earth with my knuckle. It sounded hollow. It was dry as rubber. Eons of drought. No rain for fifteen days. No rain. It has never rained. It will never rain. Heat and no wind all day long better say hot September. The year has progressed. Up one street down another. It is still September. Down one street, up another. Still September. Yesterday was the twenty second. Today is the twenty first. Impossible. Not if it was last year. But then it wouldn't be yesterday. A year is not as yesterday in his eyes. Besides last year it rained in the early part of the month. That makes a difference. It rained on the white goldenrod. Today being misplaced as against last year makes it seem better to have white—Such is progress. Yet if there is to be a novel one must begin somewhere.

Words are not permanent unless the graphite be scraped up and put in a tube or the ink lifted. Words progress into the ground. One must begin with words if one is to write. But what then of smell? What then of the hair on the trees or the golden brown cherries under the black cliffs. What of the weakness of smiles that leave dimples as much as to say : forgive me—I am slipping, slipping, slipping into nothing at all. Now I am not what I was when the word was forming to say what I am. I sit so on my bicycle and look at you greyly, dimpling because it is September and I am older than I was. I have nothing to say this minute. I shall never have anything to do unless there is progress, unless you write a novel. But if you take me in your arms—why the bicycle will fall and it will not be what it is now to smile greyly and a dimple is so deep—you might fall in and never, never remember to write a word to say good-bye to your cherries. For it is September. Begin with September.

To progress from word to word is to suck a nipple. Imagine saying : My dear, I am thirsty, will you let me have a little milk—This to love at first sight. But who do you think I am, says white goldenrod? Of course there is progress. Of course there are words. But I am thirsty, one might add. Yes but I love you and besides I have no milk. Oh yes, that is right. I forgot that we were speaking of words. Yet you cannot deny that to have a novel one must have milk. Not at the beginning. Granted, but at the end at least. Yes, yes, at the end. Progress from the mere form to the substance. Yes, yes, in other words : milk. Milk is the answer.

But how have milk out of white goldenrod? Why, that was what the Indians said. The bosom of the earth sprays up a girl balancing, balancing on a bicycle. Rapidly she passes through the first—the second eight years. Progress, you note. But September was rainy last year and how can it ever be dry again unless one go back to the year before that. There are no words. It cannot be any otherwise than as this is built the bosom of the earth shrinks back ; phosphates. Yet to have a novel— Oh catch up a dozen good smelly names and find some reason for murder, it will do. But can you not see, can you not taste, can you not smell, can you not hear, can you not touch—words? It is words that must progress. Words, white goldenrod, it is words you are made out of—THAT is why you want what you haven't got.

Progress is to get. But how can words get.—Let them get drunk. Bah. Words are words. Fog of words. The car runs through it. The words take up the smell of the car. Petrol. Face powder, arm pits, food-grease in the hair, foul breath, clean musk. Words. Words cannot progress. There cannot be a novel. Break the words. Words are indivisible crystals. One cannot break them—Awu tsst grang splith gra pragh og bm—Yes, one can break them. One can make words. Progress? If I make a word I make myself into a word. Such is progress. I shall make myself into a word. One big word. One big union. Such is progress. It is a novel. I begin small and make myself into a big splurging word : I take life and make it into one big blurb. I begin at my childhood. I begin at the beginning and make one big—Bah.

What difference is it whether I make the words or take the words. It makes no difference whatever.

There cannot be a novel. There can only be pyramids, pyramids of words, tombs. Their warm breasts heave up and down calling for a head to progress toward them, to fly onward, upon a word that was a pumpkin, now a fairy chariot, and all the time the thing was rolling backward to the time when one believed. Hans Anderson didn't believe. He had to pretend to believe. It is a conspiracy against childhood. It runs backward. Words are the reverse motion. Words are the flesh of yesterday. Words roll, spin, flare up, rumble, trickle, foam— Slowly they lose momentum. Slowly they cease to stir. At last they break up into their letters—Out of them jumps the worm that was—His hairy feet tremble upon them.

Leaving the meeting room where the Mosquito Extermination Commission had been holding an important fall conference they walked out on to the portico of the County Court House Annex where for a moment they remained in the shadow cast by the moon. A fog had arisen in which the egg-shaped white moon was fixed—so it seemed. They walked around the side of the old-fashioned wooden building—constructed in the style of the fine residences of sixty years ago and coming to the car he said : Go around that side as I will have to get in here by the wheel. The seat was wet with dew and cold—after the exceptionally hot day, They sat on it nevertheless. The windshield was opaque with the water in minute droplets on it—through which the moon shone with its inadequate light. That is, our eyes

[11]

being used to the sun the moon's light is inadequate for us to see by. But certain bats and owls find it even too strong, preferring the starlight. The stars also were out.

Turning into the exit of the parking space he stopped the car and began to wipe the wind-shield with his hand. Take this rag said the other, with one hand already in his trowser pocket. So the glass was wiped on both sides, the top and the bottom pane and the cloth—which looked a good deal like a handkerchief—was returned to the owner—who put it back where it came from not seeming to mind that it was wet and dirty. But of course the man is a mechanic in a certain sense and doesn't care.

On the highway they began to encounter the fog. It seemed in the rush of the car to come and meet them. It came suddenly, with a rush and in a moment nothing could be seen but the white billows of water crossed in front by the flares of the headlights. And so it went all the way home, sometimes clearer, sometimes so thick he had to stop, nearly — ending in his own bed-room with his wife's head on the pillow in the perfectly clear electric light. The light shone brightest on the corner of her right eye, which was nearest it, also on the prominences of her face.

Her right arm was under her head. She had been reading. The magazine Vanity Fair, which he had bought thinking of her, lay open on the coverlet. He looked at her and she at him. He smiled and she, from long practice, began to read him, progressing rapidly until she said : You can't fool me.

He became very angry but understood at once that she had penetrated his mystery, that she saw he was stealing in order to write words. She smiled again knowingly. He became furious.

CHAPTER II.

'M NEW, said she, I don't think you'll find my card here. You're new; how interesting. Can you read the letters on that chart? Open your mouth. Breathe. Do you have headaches? No. Ah, yes, you are new. I'm new, said the oval moon at the bottom of the mist funnel, brightening and paling. I don't think you'll find my card there. Open your mouth — Breathe — A crater big enough to hold the land from New York to Philadelphia. New! I'm new, said the quartz crystal on the parlor table — like glass — Mr. Tiffany bought a cart load of them. Like water or white rock candy — I'm new, said the mist rising from the duck pond, rising, curling, turning under the moon — Unknown grasses asleep in the level mists, pieces of the fog. Last night it was an ocean. Tonight trees. Already it is yesterday. Turned into the wrong street seeking to pass the power house from which the hum, hmmmmmmmmmmmmm — sprang. Electricity has been discovered for ever. I'm new, says the great dynamo. I am progress. I make a word. Listen! UMMM-MMMMMMMMM —

Ummmmmmmmmmm — Turned into the wrong street at three A.M. lost in the fog, listening, searching — Waaaa! said the baby. I'm new. A boy! A what? Boy. Shit, said the father of two other sons. Listen here. This is no place to talk that way. What a word to use. I'm new, said the sudden word.

The fog lay in deep masses on the roads at three A.M. Into the wrong street turned the car seeking the high pitched singing tone of the dynamos endlessly spinning in the high banquet hall, filling the house and the room where the bed of pain stood with progress. Ow, ow! Oh help me somebody ! said she. UMMMMMM sang the dynamo in the next street, UMMMM. With a terrible scream she drowned out its sound. He went to the window to see if his car was still there, pulled the curtain aside, green — Yes it was still there under the light where it would not be so likely to be struck by other cars coming in the fog. There it was as still as if it were asleep. Still as could be. Not a wheel moved. No sound came from the engine. It stood there under the purple arc-light, partly hidden by a pole which cast a shadow toward him in the masses of floating vapor. He could see the redtail-light still burning brightly with the electricity that came from the battery under the floor boards. No one had stolen the spare tire. It was very late. — Well, said he, dropping the shade and thinking that maybe when he was busy someone might easily come up from the meadows and take the spare tire — Well, I suppose I had better see how things have progressed.

And so he backed out into the main street and turned up another block. And there he saw. The great doors were open to full view of the world. A great amphitheatre of mist lighted from the interior of the power house. In rows sat the great black machines saying vrummmmmmmmmmmmmmmm. Stately in the great hall they sat and generated electricity to light the cellar stairs with. To warm the pad on Mrs. Voorman's belly. To cook supper by and iron Abie's pyjamas. Here was democracy. Here is progress — here is the substance of words — UMMMMM: that is to say meat or linen or belly ache. — Three A.M. To be exact twenty-eight minutes past three.

And all this was yesterday — Yesterday and there at her window I saw her, the lady of my dreams her long and sallow face, held heavily near the glass, overlooking the street where the decayed-meat wagon passes and the ice-cream cart rumbles with its great power and the complicated affairs of the town twitter toward the open sewer in the meadows by the Button Factory. Orange peel, tomato peel floating in a whitish, soapy flow — Her face without expression, the lady I am dying for, her right shoulder as high as her ear, the line of the shoulder sloping down acutely to the neck, her left shoulder also raised so that her head seemed to lie loose in a kind of saddle.

Supreme in stupidity and a fog of waste, profit in what is left. Oh what delectable morsel is left. Blessed hunchback, scum of loves weekly praying in all churches — which by the way take up the very best sites in the town. There she sat, her body low down below the window frame, only her face showing, and looked at me dully, looked because I looked — and my heart leaped up to her in passionate appeal that she

should be my queen and run with me over the foggy land —
Forward — Onward and upward forever.

So saying the day had progressed toward the afternoon
and under the poplars the dried leaves had begun to collect.
It had been unbearably hot. September is a hot month. The
leaves had fallen one by one. No wind. One by one pushed
off by the buds which swollen by the heat had thought that
winter was over. Off with you. You stand in the way of
progress, say the young leaves. Sitting on his chair he seemed
like any other man but to get to the bed he suddenly descended
to the floor. On his long arms — he Apollo, and using the
stumps of his legs, apelike on all fours and talking quietly he
swung himself up over the edge of the bed and lay down.

Over the field — for the fog had left the grasses in the early
morning when the sun came up with majestic progression,
haughtily leaving the dropping city under him — over the field —
for it was late in the afternoon and the sunlight shone in with
his poor broken legs, crippled as he was — the sun shone in from
the west. The car had turned in to the wrong street and he
had gone into the store where the paralysed Scotchman whom
he had never seen before put him on the way — climbing into his
bed sent his rays almost level over a patch of red grass hot and
blinding. Over the field the heat rose and in it even from a
distance due to the blur of light on their wings a great swarm
of gnats could be seen turning, twisting in the air, rising falling —
over the grass, fringed with the progressing sun.

But with great sweeps and sudden turns a dozen dragon
flies seeming twice as large as they really were, from the sun
blurring their transparent wings, darted back and forth over the
field catching and eating the gnats. Swiftly the gnats progressed
into the dragon flies, swiftly coalescing — and from time to time
a droplet of stuff fell from the vent of a feeding dragon fly, —
and the little sound of this stuff striking the earth could not be
heard with its true poetic force. Lost. Lost in a complicated
world. Except in the eyes of God. But a word, a word rang true.
Shit, said the father. With this name I thee christen : he added
under his breath.

And yet — one must begin somewhere.

Deeply religious, he walked into the back yard and watching

lest the children see him and want what they shouldn't have he approached the grape vines. Selecting a bunch of Delawares he picked it with some difficulty spilling a few of the fruit. Then he walked to the other side and found some blue ones. These too he ate. Then some white which he ate also one by one swallowing the pulp and the seeds and spitting out the skins. He continued to eat but no word came to satisfy.

Somehow a word must be found. He felt rather a weight in his belly from eating so many grapes. He, himself that must die someday, he the deeply religious friend of great men and women in incipience, he couldn't find a word. Only words and words. He ate another bunch of the grapes. More words. And never THE word.

A novel must progress toward a word. Any word that — Any word. There is an idea.

His brother was ill. He must go home. The sun will soon be on the Pacific coast. To bed, to bed — take off the clothes beginning on the outside and working in. How would it be to take off the underwear first, then the shirt —

Progress is dam foolishness. — It is a game. Either I have or — a thieves' game. Hold me close, closer, close as you can. I can't hold you any closer. I have been stealing. I should never touch anything. I should never think of anything but you. I love another. It is a word. I have left you alone to run wild with a girl. I would be tame. Lies flicker in the sun. Visions beset noonday. Through the back window of the shoe-shine parlor a mass of golden glow flashes in the heat. Come into my heart while I am running — jumping from airplane to plane in mid-air. I cannot stop : the word I am seeking is in your mouth — I cannot stop. Hold me against —

You are wrong, wrong Alva N. Turner. It is deeper than you imagine. I perceive that it may be permissible for a poet to write about a poetic sweetheart but never about a wife — should have said possible. It is not possible. All men do the same. Dante be damned. Knew nothing at all. Lied to himself all his life. Profited by his luck and never said thanks. God pulled the lady up by the roots. Never even said thank you. Quite wrong. Look what he produced. Page after page. Helped the world to bread. Have another slice of bread

Mr. Helseth.   No thank you — Not hungry tonight?   Something on his mind.

The word.   Who.

Liberate the words. You tie them. Poetic sweet-heart. Ugh. Poetic sweetheart. My dear Miss Word let me hold your W. I love you. Of all the girls in school you alone are the one —

Dramatise myself make it sing together as if the world were a bird who married to the same mate five years understood in the end transmigration of souls.

Nonsense. I am a writer and will never be anything else. In which case it is impossible to find the word. But to have a novel one must progress with the words. The words must become real, they must take the place of wife and sweet-heart. They must be church — Wife. It must be your wife. It must be a thing of adamant with the texture of wind. Wife.

Am I a word? Words, words, words —

And approaching the end of the novel in his mind as he sat there with his wife sleeping alone in the next room he could feel that something unusual had happened. Something had grown up in his life dearer than — It, as the end. The words from long practice had come to be leaves, trees, the corners of his house — such was the end. He had progressed leaving the others far behind him. Alone in that air with the words of his brain he had breathed again the pure mountain air of joy — there night after night in his poor room. And now he must leave her. She the — He had written the last word and getting up he understood the fog as it billowed before the lights.

That which had been impossible for him at first had become possible. Everything had been removed that other men had tied to the words to secure them to themselves. Clean, clean he had taken each word and made it new for himself so that at last it was new, free from the world for himself — never to touch it — dreams of his babyhood — poetic sweetheart. No. He went in to his wife with exalted mind, his breath coming in pleasant surges. I come to tell you that the book is finished.

I have added a new chapter to the art of writing. I feel sincerely that all they say of me is true, that I am truly a great man and a great poet.

What did you say, dear, I have been asleep?

CHAPTER III.

IT IS JOYCE with a difference. The difference being greater opacity, less erudition, reduced power of perception — Si la sol fa mi re do. Aside from that simple, rather stupid derivation, forced to a ridiculous extreme. No excuse for this sort of thing. Amounts to a total occlusion of intelligence. Substitution of something else. What? Well, nonsense. Since you drive me to it.

Take the improvisations : What the French reader would say is : *Oui, ça ; j'ai déjà vu ça ; ça c'est de Rimbaud.* Finis.

Representative American verse will be that which will appear new to the French . . . . prose the same.

Infertile Joyce laments the failure of his sterile pen. Siegfried Wagner runs to his Mama crying : Mutti, Mutti, listen, I have just composed a beautiful Cantata on a theme I discovered in one of father's operas.

In other words it comes after Joyce, therefore it is no good, of no use but a secondary local usefulness like the Madison Square Garden tower copied from Seville — It is of no absolute good. It is not NEW. It is not an invention.

Invention, I want to buy you some clothes. Now what would you really like to have? Let us pretend we have no intelligence whatever, that we have read ALL there is to read and that Rimbaud has taught us nothing, that Joyce has passed in a cloud, that, in short, we find nothing to do but begin with Macaulay or King James, that all writing is forbidden us save that which we recognise to be inadequate. NOW show your originality, *mon ami.* NOW let me see what you can do with your vaunted pen.

Nothing could be easier.

My invention this time, my dear, is that literature is a pure matter of words. The moon making a false star of the weather vane on the steeple makes also a word. You do not know the fine hairs on a hickory leaf? Try one in the woods some time. You will grasp at once what I mean.

But Joyce. He is misjudged, misunderstood. His vaunted invention is a fragile fog. His method escapes him. He has not the slightest notion what he is about. He is a priest, a roysterer of the spirit. He is an epicurean of romance. His true genius flickers and fails: there's the peak, there in the trees — For God's sake can't you see it! Not that tree but the mass of rocks, that reddish mass of rocks, granite, with the sun on it between that oak and the maple. — That is not an oak. Hell take it what's the use of arguing with a botanist.

But I will not have my toothpicks made of anything but maple. Mr. Joyce will you see to it that my toothpicks are not made of anything but maple? Irish maple. Damn it, it's for Ireland. Pick your teeth, God knows you need to. The trouble with writing of the old style is that the teeth don't fit. They were made for Irishmen — as a class.

Tell me now, of what in your opinion does Mr. Joyce's art consist, since you have gone so far as to criticise the teeth he makes? — Why, my dear, his art consists of words.

What then is his failure, O God. — His failure is when he mistakes his art to be something else.

What then does he mistake his art to be, Rosinante? — He mistakes it to be several things in more or less certain rotation from botany — Oh well it's a kind of botany you know — from botany to — to — litany. Do you know his poetry?

But you must not mistake his real, if hidden, service. He has in some measure liberated words, freed them for their proper uses. He has to a great measure destroyed what is known as "literature." For me as an American it is his only important service.

It would be a pity if the French failed to discover him for a decade or so. Now wouldn't it? Think how literature would suffer. Yes think — think how LITERATURE would suffer.

At that the car jumped forward like a live thing. Up the steep board incline into the garage it leaped — as well as a thing on four wheels could leap — But with great dexterity he threw out the clutch with a slight pressure of his left foot, just as the fore end of the car was about to career against a mass of old window screens at the garage end. Then pressing with his right foot and grasping the hand-brake he brought the machine to a halt — just in time — though it was no trick to him, he having done it so often for the past ten years.

It seemed glad to be at home in its own little house, the trusty mechanism. The lights continued to flare intimately against the wooden wall as much as to say : Here I am back again. The engine sighed and stopped at the twist of the key governing the electric switch. Out went the lights with another twist of the wrist. The owner groped his way to the little door at the back and emerged into the moonlight, into the fog, leaving his idle car behind him to its own thoughts. There it must remain all night, requiring no food, no water to drink, nothing while he, being a man, must live. His wife was at the window holding the shade aside.

And what is good poetry made of
And what is good poetry made of
Of rats and snails and puppy-dog's tails
And that is what good poetry is made of

And what is bad poetry made of
And what is bad poetry made of
Of sugar and spice and everything nice
That is what bad poetry is made of

A Rebours : Huysman puts it. My dear let us free ourselves from this enslavement. We do not know how thoroughly we are bound. It must be a new definition, it must cut us off from the rest. It is in a different line. Good morning Boss said the old colored man working on the railroad and started to sing : Jesus, Jesus I love you. It was Sunday, he was working on the railroad on Sunday and had to put up some barrier. It is an end to art temporarily. That upstart Luther. My God don't talk to me of Luther, never changed his bed clothes for a year. Well, my dear, IT'S COMING just the same. To hell with art. To hell with literature. The old renaissance priests guarded art in their cloisters for three hundred years or more. Sunk their teeth in it. The ONE solid thing. Don't blame me if it went down with them. DOWN, you understand. Fist through the middle of the rose window. You are horror struck. One word : Bing! One accurate word and a shower of colored glass following it. Is it MY fault? Ask the French if that is literature.

Do you mean to say that art — O ha, ha. Do you mean to say that art— O ha, ha. Well spit it out. Do you mean to say that art is SERIOUS? — Yes. Do you mean to say that art does any WORK? — Yes. Do you mean — ? Revolution. Russia. Kropotkin. Farm, Factory and Field. — CRRRRRRASH. — Down comes the world. There you are gentlemen, I am an artist.

What then would you say of the usual interpretation of the word "literature"? — Permanence. A great army with its tail in antiquity. Cliché of the soul : beauty.

But can you have literature without beauty? It all depends on what you mean by beauty.

There is beauty in the bellow of the BLAST, etc. from all previous significance. — To me beauty is purity. To me it is discovery, a race on the ground.

And for this you are willing to smash —

Yes, everything. — To go down into hell. — Well let's look.

CHAPTER IV.

HAT'S all very fine about *le mot juste* but first the word must be free. — But is there not some other way? It must come about gradually. Why go down into hell when — Because words are not men, they have no adjustments that need to be made. They are words. They can not be anything but free or bound. Go about it any way you chose.

The word is the thing. If it is smeared with colors from right and left what can it amount to?

I'd hate to have to live up there, she said with a frown. It was the soul that spoke. In her words could be read the whole of democracy, the entire life of the planet. It fell by chance on his ear but he was ready, he was alert.

And the little dusty car : There drawn up at the gutter was a great truck painted green and red. Close to it passed the little runabout while conscious desire surged in its breast. Yes there he was the great powerful mechanism, all in his new paint against the gutter while she rolled by and saw — The Polish woman in the clinic, yellow hair slicked back. Neck, arms, breast, waist, hips, etc. This is THE thing — The small mechanism went swiftly by the great truck with fluttering heart in the hope, the secret hope that perhaps, somehow he would notice — HE, the great truck in his massiveness and paint, that somehow he would come to her. Oh I wouldn't like to live up there!

FOG HOLDS UP LINERS say the head lines. It is a blackness, a choking smother of dirty water in suspension. — You should have been here this morning. You could look out and see nothing but a sea of cloud below us. Right at our feet the fog began and stretched off as far as the eye could perceive.

Up out of the trees with a whirr started the sparrows. With a loud clatter the grouse got up at his feet. The ground was full of mushrooms. Everything, no matter what it is must be re-valuated.

The red grass will soon open into feathers.

Peter Broom, yes sah, my grandfather sah, the greatest man in Prince George County. He had three hundred children.

So many things, so many things : heat.

What then are you trying to say in THIS chapter? And what of your quest of THE word? What of A.N.T. ant?

Why someone has offended Wells. He has retorted with NEO-ACADEMICIAN : And : No new form of the novel required. Lack of substance always takes the form of novelty mongering. Empire must be saved! Saved for the proletariat.

On the side of the great machine it read : Standard Motor Gasoline, in capital letters. A great green tank was built upon the red chassis, FULL of gas. The little car looked and her heart leaped with shy wonder.

Save the words. Save the words from themselves. They are like children. Young Men's Hebrew Association. Save them while they're still young. Words must not be allowed to say, to do — Geld them. They are not REALLY words they are geldings. Save the words. Yes, I repeat SAVE THE WORDS. When Voronoff would have had words to transplant, interstitial words — he said save the words.

And what has anything Wells says to do with serious writing. FIRST let the words be free. The words are men, therefore they are not men. They cannot, must not, will not be mustered of the people, by the people, for the people. They are words. They will have their way.

Puh, puh, puh, puh! said the little car going up hill. But the great green and red truck said nothing but continued to discharge its gasolene into a tank buried in the ground near the gutter.

And the fog had coalesced into rain. Rain to soak the firewood the boys had left beside their old fire, like good scouts, for those to come after and the great car continued to discharge.

CHAPTER V.

HAT then is a novel? *Un Novello*, pretty, pretty Baby. It is a thing of fixed form. It is pure English. Yes, she is of Massachusetts stock. Her great grandfather was thrown out of the Quaker church for joining the Continental army. Hates the English. Her life is a novel — almost too sensational.

The story of Miss Li — so well told.

Qu'avez-vous vu? Or they that write much and see little. Not much use to us.

Speak of old Sun Bow pacing his mesa instead of Felipe Segundo in the barren halls of El Escorial — or asleep in his hard bed at one corner of the griddle.

My mother would have a little nigger boy come with a brush and sit at her feet and brush her legs by the hour.

Expressionism is to express skilfully the seething reactions of the contemporary European consciousness. Cornucopia. In at the small end and — blui! Kandinsky.

But it's a fine thing. It is THE thing for the moment — in Europe. The same sort of thing, reversed, in America has a water attachment to be released with a button. That IS art. Everyone agrees that that IS art. Just as one uses a handkerchief.

It is the apotheosis of relief. Dadaism in one of its prettiest modes : *rien*, *rien*, *rien*.— But wait a bit. Maybe Dadaism is not so weak as one might imagine. — One takes it for granted almost without a thought that expressionism is the release of SOMETHING. Now then Aemilius, what is European consciousness composed of? — Tell me in one word. — *Rien*, *rien*, *rien*! It is at least very complicated. Oh very.

You damned jackass. What do you know about Europe? Yes, what in Christ's name do you know? Your mouth is a sewer, a cloaca.

Complicated consciousness quite aside from a possible revaluation. It has no value for ME. It is all very interesting and God knows we have enough to learn. The swarming European consciousness. But there it is much simpler — No good to us.

Swarming European consciousness : Kreisler and Ysaye were the only ones with any value. They had a few pennies over and above expenses. They swarm here now for something to eat. But the funniest are the ones from Russia ; each excoriates the playing of the other and calls the other a Sheeny. Wow!

Really you are too naive. They are merely reacting to the American atmosphere — It is their work that counts. And besides a virtuoso is not really creative in any serious sense. Would a great artist, say Kandinsky — ? In any case it all seems to preoccupy you so, and in a book about America, really —

Take their work. I resent it all. I hate every symphony, every opera as much as a nigger should hate *Il Trovatore*. Not perhaps hate it in a purely aesthetic sense but from under. It is an impertinence. Where in God's name is our Alexander to cut, cut, cut, throught this knot.

Europe is nothing to us. Simply nothing. Their music is death to us. We are starving — not dying — not dying mind you — but lean-bellied for words. God I would like to see some man, some one of the singers step out in the midst of some one of Aida's songs and scream like a puma.

But you poor fellow, you use such inept figures. Aida has been dead artistically in Munich for fifty years.

Wagner then — Strauss. It is no difference to me. Tear it all apart. Start with one note. One word. Chant it over and over forty different ways.

But it would be stupid —

It would, if it were what I mean — it would be accurate. It would articulate with something. It would signify relief. Release I mean. It would be the beginning.

Do not imagine I do not see the necessity of learning from Europe — or China but we will learn what we will, and never what they would teach us. America is a mass of pulp, a jelly, a sensitive plate ready to take whatever print you want to put on it — We have no art, no manners, no intellect — we have nothing. We water at the eyes at our own stupidity. We have only mass movement like a sea. But we are not a sea —

Europe we must — We have no words. Every word we get must be broken off from the European mass. Every word we get placed over again by some delicate hand. Piece by piece we must loosen what we want. What we will have. Will they let it go? Hugh.

I touch the words and they baffle me. I turn them over in my mind and look at them but they mean little that is clean. They are plastered with muck out of the cities. —

We must imitate the motivation and shun the result.

We are very few to your many —

But what is all this but waste energy.

No it is not. It is as near as I can come for the present to the word. What good to talk to me of Santayana and your later critics. I brush them aside. They do not apply. They do not reach me any more than a baby's hand reaches the moon. I am far under them. I am less, far less if you will. I am a beginner. I am an American. A United Stateser. Yes its ugly, there is no word to say it better. I do not believe in ugliness. I do not want to call myself a United Stateser but what in — but what else am I? Ugliness is a horror to me but it is less abhorrent than to be like you even in the most remote, the most minute particular. For the moment I hate you, I hate your orchestras, your libraries, your sciences, your yearly salons, your finely tuned intelligences of all sorts. My intelligence is as finely tuned as yours but it lives in hell, it is doomed to eternal — perhaps eternal — shiftings after what? Oh to hell with Masters and the rest of them. To hell with everything I have myself ever written.

Here's a man wants me to revise, to put in order. My God what I am doing means just the opposite from that. There is no revision, there can be no revision —

Down came the rain with a crash. For five days it had been pending. With a loud splash it seemed to strike the earth as if it were body meeting body. The poplar leaves swirled and swirled. The gutters were wedged with water.

Oh fool you are thicker than rain drops.

Give me to Moussorgsky. I am tired. Take me to the opera tonight and let me see Nijinsky dance his *Til Eulenspiegel* for I am tired to death with looking for sense among American

[26]

poets. Igor will retrieve my courage. I could sit and listen in his lap for ever. Were not the American Indians Mongols? Oh they must have been. Why could they not have been Chinese? Why could not the early Emperors have discovered America? Tell me, wet streets, what we are coming to, we in this country? Are we doomed? Must we be another Europe or another Japan with our coats copied from China, another bastard country in a world of bastards? Is this our doom or will we ever amount to anything?

Drown me in pictures like Marsden, make me a radical artist in the conventional sense. Give me the intelligence of a Wells. God, Hueffer is so far beyond him that what Wells says really sounds sensible.

Must it be a civilisation of fatigued spirits? Then give me Hueffer. My God it is too disgusting.

Great men of America! O very great men of America please lend me a penny so I wont have to go to the opera.

Why not capitalise Barnum —?

Bravo, bravo mon vieux! A noble apostrophe to your country but don't you realise that it is not a matter of country but the time — The time.

For God's sake Charlie bring a lemon pie.

So they lay in the little brook and let the cold water run up their bare bellies.

CHAPTER VI.

IN SPITE of the moon in mid sky and the plaster of dully shining leaves on the macadam and all the other signs of the approach of fine weather there rang in his head: Such a cuddle muddle: Is that modern German poetry? I never saw such a lot of things mixed together under one title. These are modern times, Pa, airships and automobiles; you cover space —

And that's all right —

O America! Turn your head a little to the left please. So. Now are you ready? Watch my hand. Now: *Lohengrin* in ITALIAN, SUNG AT MANHATTAN — San Carlo Company Revives Wagner Opera, with Anna Fitziu as Elsa.

Sweet kisses that come in the night — O argyrol!

Rain, rain, for three days and three nights.

In the night a cesura. Suddenly the fire bell begins to ring. I wake with a start and hear the small boy calling from the next room. Eight thousand people wake and count the strokes of the black bells. It is not our signal. Someone has been set afire. The engines pass with a crash and roar of the exhausts. Their siren whistles shriek with a fortissimo rise and fall. In a thousand beds men of forty, women of thirty eight, girls in their teens, boys tired from football practice and little boys and girls down to babyhood wake and think the same thoughts. They listen and count the number of strokes, and sink back saying to themselves: Fire! Presently all but the few who are immediately affected are again asleep. The fire has burnt itself out. Slowly the sun has been crossing Europe and will soon appear fresh from the sea with his benison. The tie of that black thought in the night will be broken. The opportunity will be lost forever. Each will rise and dress and go out into the rain on whatever errand the day has chosen for him.

Rain all day long. The sun does not appear. The heat is suffocating. The rattle of the torrent fills the ears. Water is everywhere.

In the night a wind wakens. It comes from the south-west about midnight and takes the trees by their heavy leaves twisting them until they crack. With a roar the wind batters at the houses, shaking them as if it were a heavy hand. And again for the second night running eight thousand men and women and boys and girls wake and listen or get up to close windows and to look out at the trees leaning with snapping branches, tossing and seething with a sound of escaping steam. It has grown cold. Pull up the covers. It has grown cold. Sixteen thousand hands have drawn the covers closer about the bodies. The wind is cold.

The sun has come back. The air is washed clean. Leaves lie plastered upon the streets, against the tree trunks, upon the very house sides. The bird bath is filled to overflowing. A lame man is hurrying for the train.

They had talked for hours. The new project was beginning to take form. It was the evening of the second day. There stood the train puffing out great volumes of dense smoke which no sooner arose than it was caught in the wind and sent flying out ahead of the train. I wish to God I were on that train wherever it might be going. Oh well, remarked the younger man and said good-bye, which is what it is to be a man.

He was too old, remarked the voice in the room next to the one in which the woman was lying, he never should have gone out in that rain. Too cold! At times it seems possible, even now. She took the hair between her thumb and index finger of the right hand and using her left hand swiftly stroked the little hair strands back toward the head to make it stand out. Ratting it, I told her. It ruins the hair. Oh well I haven't much left, it might as well be broken.

She wore blue stockings under a very quiet dress but the world has not beheld a more maddening spectacle. Devoted to the art of writing, he read with his mind watching her and his mind in the sky seeking, seeking some earth to stand on when the boys were tearing up the soggy turf with their cleats. What to do? There it is. The wind hesitated whether or not to impregnate her. So many things were to be considered. In the years since his passage over Ponce de Leon's soldiers on the beach — the wind footloose, gnawing the leaves had witnessed flying footballs that it had blown out of bounds. He had not a word to stand on, yet he stood, not knowing why. Fear clutched his heart. Visions of uprooted trees passed over his heart as he shook her heavy skirt about her knees. But she, oblivious to it all, walked with downcast eyes — looking at her feet or smiling pleasantly at one here and there in the crowd that was shouting and pressing to see the players.

In the night all nature was asleep as she lay with her young cheek pressed against her pillow and slept. The boys tossed and turned from the stiffness in their joints and from the bruises received in the game. But she lay quiet and asleep, the breath coming slowly in regular flow from her hollow nostrils moving them slightly back and forth.

Under the covers her young form could be made out, the left shoulder, the hips and the legs and feet, the left knee slightly bent and fallen to the mattress before the other. Not a sound in the room for a million years. Still she lay there asleep. — The wind has turned into hail.

Spring flowers are blossoming in the wind. There is the tulip, the jonquil and the violet — for it is September and no man shall know his defeat. So there are spring flowers that grew up through the ice that will be present later. It is of ice that they have made the flowers.

Yet sometimes it seems that it would still be possible. And this is romance : to believe that which is unbelievable. This is faith : to desire that which is never to be obtained, to ride like a swallow on the wind — apparently for the pleasure of flight.

The swallow's bill is constructed in such a way that in flying with his mouth open tiny insects that enter are ensnared in hair-like gills so that he is fed.

Here are a pretty pair of legs in blue stockings, feed. Yet without the thought of a possible achievement that would make it possible to command the achievement of certain — The boys kick the ball and pay no attention. The boys kick the ball up into the wind and the wind hurriedly writes a love note upon it : Meet me tonight. Say you are going to the Library and I will have my car at the corner of Fern Street. I have something to tell you. There is one word you must hear : YOU.

There is one word you must hear. It will come out at my

lips and enter in at your ears. It might be written with letters on white paper but it is a word that I want you to have out of the lips into your ear. And she answers: I will be there. So he does not keep his appointment. Off he goes in search of a word.

But she goes home and weeps her eyes out. Her pillow is wet with her tears —

What do you think! He has left his wife, and a child in the high school has been ill a week, weeping her eyes out and murmuring his name. Is it not terrible?

It is the wind! The wind is in the poplars twiddling the fading leaves between his fingers idly and thinking, thinking of the words he will make, new words to be written on white paper but never to be spoken by the lips to pass into her ear.

Quietly he goes home to his wife and taking her by the shoulder wakes her: Here I am.

CHAPTER VII.

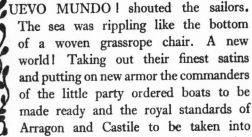

UEVO MUNDO! shouted the sailors. The sea was rippling like the bottom of a woven grassrope chair. A new world! Taking out their finest satins and putting on new armor the commanders of the little party ordered boats to be made ready and the royal standards of Arragon and Castile to be taken into them. The men meanwhile feeling the balmy air and seeing green and a shore for the first time in two months were greedily talking of fresh fruit — after their monotonous and meager diet of meat — of milk, of a chance to walk free in the air, to escape their commanders, and of women. Yes perhaps there would be women, beautiful savages of manifold charms. But most of all they were filled with the wild joy of release from torment of the mind. For not one among them but expected to be eaten by a god or a monster long since or to have been boiled alive by a hypertropical sea. Excitedly they went down the ladders and took their places at the words of the boatswain spoken in the Castilian tongue.

Of Columbus' small talk on that occasion nothing remains but it could not have been of Eric the Discoverer. Nor of the parties of Asiatics and Islanders — Pacific Islanders who had in other ages peopled the continents from the east. No matter : *Nuevo Mundo*! had shouted the sailors and *Nuevo Mundo* it was sure enough as they found out as soon as they had set foot on it and Columbus had kneeled and said prayers and the priest had spoken his rigmarole in the name of Christ and the land was finally declared taken over for Ferdinand and Isabella the far distant king and queen.

Yes it was indeed a new world. They the product of an age-long civilization beginning in India, it is said, and growing through conquest and struggle of all imaginable sorts through periods of success and decline, through ages of walkings to and fro in the fields and woods and the streets of cities that were without walls and had walls and burst their walls and became ruins again ; through the changes of speech : Sanscrit, Greek, Latin growing crooked in the mouths of peasants who would rise and impose their speech on their masters, and on divisions in the state and savage colonial influences, words accurate to the country, Italian, French and Spanish itself not to speak of Portuguese. Words! Yes this party of sailors, men of the sea, brothers of a most ancient guild, ambassadors of all the ages that had gone before them, had indeed found a new world, a world, that is, that knew nothing about them, on which the foot of a white man had never made a mark such as theirs were then making on the white sand under the palms. *Nuevo Mundo*!

The children released from school lay in the gutter and covered themselves with the fallen poplar leaves.—A new world! All summer the leaves had been thick on the branches but now after the heat and the rain and the wind the branches were beginning to be bare. More sky appeared to their eyes than ever before. With what relief the children had pranced in the wind! Now they lay half covered in the leaves and enjoying the warmth looked out on the new world.

And he was passing and saw them. And wondered if it were too late to be Eric. What a new world they had made of it with their Cortezes, their Pizarros yes and their Lord Howes, . their Washingtons even. The Declaration of Independence. I wonder, he said, whether it could be possible that the influence of the climate — I wonder if the seed, the sperm of that, existed in Columbus. Was it authentic? Is there a word to be found there? Could it be that in those men who had crossed, in the Norse as well as the Mongols, something spontaneous could not have been implanted out of the air? Or was the declaration to be put to the credit of that German George? Was it only the result of local conditions?

"A new declaration of independence, signed by Columbus, found in Porto Rico."

Indians in any case, pale yellow and with lank black hair came to the edge of the bushes and stared : The Yaquis territory lay north of the river Fuertes. To the south was Carrancista territory. The valley was fertile, the Indians wanted it.

During the week of November 13th, 17th, 1916 — word

reached Los Mochis that Gen. Banderas and the Villistas from Chihuahua had been defeated by the Carrancistas near Fuertes and were in retreat. During this week two Indians were captured by Los Mochis police and hung on willow trees below the Jaula.

On Saturday November 13th, Col. Escobar and his Carrancistas of the Fifth regiment of Sinaloa were withdrawn from Los Mochis and Aguila and concentrated in San Blas. Banderas and his Villistas meanwhile had come down the Fuertes, effected a junction with Bachomo and his Mayo Indians, and Monday night crossed the river above Los Tastos, tore out the telephone at the pumps and started for Los Mochis. All gate keepers encountered on the road were killed as were their families. Mr. Wilcox estimated the combined forces participating in the raid and on the other side of the river at 6,000.

The first intimation of the raid was at one o'clock in the morning of Tuesday when with a *"Villa! Vive Villa! Vive Villa!"* the raiders swarmed into Los Mochis from three sides, shooting cursing as they galloped into town. From all over the town came the sound of smashing doors and windows, shots, yells and screams.

When I came here the Indians all used bows and arrows. Conscripted during the many revolutions they had deserted with their rifles until at last, after 800 of them, in a body, went over they used the rifle extensively. Wilcox lived at the pumps with his wife and daughter. A cocky Englishman, he poopooed the danger. He had been in the habit of telephoning into the town, seven miles, whenever a raid was coming. It was agreed we Americans were to keep to our houses, take our animals off the roads and wait with more or less excitement until it was over. We never notified the Mexicans. Had we done so once we should not have escaped the next raid. This time the Villistas were with the Indians. As you saw the first thing they did was to rip out the wires. Washington had just accepted Carranza as the power in authority and the Villistas were angry.

Wilcox and his wife and daughter were locked in a room all the first night while Banderas and Bacomo argued over their fate. Banderas was for killing Wilcox and taking over his wife and daughter for camp women. But the Indian stood out against him. It seems Wilcox had at one time given the Indians some sacks of beans when they were hard up for food. They remembered this. It was a good thing for the three.

At a previous raid an American engineer living near Wilcox was found dead. He was supposed to have run. Looked just like a pin-cushion, with the feathered arrows that were in him. Funniest thing you ever saw in your life. There were four bullets in him also.

The Americans were too scattered to resist. It was decided to save the few guns by hiding them. Bacomo rode up to the house with his escort, — ordered to give up all guns and cartridges. At the last moment he turned back from the stairs, entered Mrs. Johnson's room where the ladies were sitting on the beds and ordered them to get up. Under the mattress a miscellaneous collection of riot guns, rifles, shot guns, automatics, pistols and cartridges were found. When all the guns and cartridges to the last shell had been loaded on the horses behind the drunken soldiers Bacomo refused C.'s request for one of the riot guns and with a polite bow and a *"Con permiso, senores,"* he rode off.

In Mr. Johnson's cellar they had found all sorts of bottles from Scotch to German *Scheiswasser* and had drunk it all indiscriminately.

Cattle had eaten the standing rice. The pigs had got loose and over-run everything. Returning there were corpses on all sides. About one of these a triple battle raged. The pigs were ranged on one side, the dogs on another and from a third a flock of vultures crept up from time to time. The pigs and dogs would make a united rush at the birds who would fly a few feet into the air and settle a yard or so away.

These pictures are of Bacomo taken a year later just as he was being taken from the train by his captors. He was a physical wreck at the time but at the time of the raid he was a magnificent specimen of a man. It seemed there was some silver buried near Los Mochis which they wanted. He would not disclose its whereabouts unless they freed him and they would not free him unless he spoke first.

The end is shown in this picture. Here he is with the pick and spade at his feet surrounded by the Carrancista soldiers. He dug his grave and was shot and they buried him there.

The Indians have made a local saint of him and every night

you will see candles burning on the spot and little plates of rice and other food placed there for his spirit. —

For a moment Columbus stood as if spell-bound by the fact of this new country. Soon however he regained his self-possession and with Alonzo Pinzon ordered the trunks of trifles to be opened which, being opened, the Indians drew near in wonder and began to try to communicate with these gods.

It was indeed a new world.

CHAPTER VIII.

O MAN can tell the truth and survive — save through prestige. And no child either. Aristocracy is license to tell the truth. And to hear it. Witness the man William in Henry Fifth, the camp incident. Fear clutched at his heart.

Agh-ha-ha! Shouted the *vaqueros* plunging their spurs into the bronchos' sides. Up with the heels. Buck, buck, buck. Agh-ha-ha! *Fortissimo*. The wild and unexpected cry out of the Mexican Indian country rang through the quiet house so that the pup leaped up and rushed to the door.

Someone had taken the apple. Both denied they had had a hand in it. Each accused the other. The truth did not appear. For an hour the man tried his best to arrive at a just decision. Joseph Smith shook where he stood and fell frothing at the mouth. He was of Vermont mountain stock. His birth among the poor white trash there had not even been thought worth recording. Yet a vision came to him of the marriage in Cana. Christ drank the wine and Martha and Mary her sister became his wives — so to speak. It is the truth. The world shall be saved anew, said Joseph Smith in the mountains of Vermont — where the mushrooms are so plentiful among the fir trees.

Who had given the boy the apple against the father's express orders? Had he taken it himself — which he denied or had the girl gone into the store room — as he asserted but which she denied — and selected it herself? Where was the truth?

In Illinois Brigham Young was recruited. Off they set with fifty oxen for the Promised Land away over the prairies and deserts — through the Sioux country, in search of Zion. The whole world they would leave behind and for the truth's sake they would live in that far country — to be discovered, to which the Lord would lead them.

Go upstairs sir and take your clothes off. You shall go to bed for this lie — I'll say I took the apple Daddy, said the boy

[37]

sobbing violently, but she gave it to me. In minute detail he repeated the story of how the apple was picked out of the basket by the girl and handed to him to eat.

Lions of the Lord. The boy would not give up his bride to Brigham and was *altered*, as a rebel. She went mad. In' 49 a party of gold seekers came by accident into the valley they had found. They were gently received. A warning was given of hostile Indians and a special guard was appointed to conduct them safely on their way. But Brigham had had a dream. Men must not wander into the valley of Zion to disturb the ways of God's holy ones. A blood sacrifice had been demanded of Brigham by the Lord. John D. Lee was selected as he who must lend himself to the Almighty will of God for the good of the church and state. Slowly the party of gold seekers departed for California. At the narrow defile at Mountain Meadow the treacherous business was performed. All but a child were killed and Brigham and the Lord were revenged. Later John D. Lee was convicted of murder by government authorities and shot. A poor ignorant tool in the hands of that most mighty Lion of the Lord.

And you my girl. You have lied to me before this. Did you or did you not take the apple? No one will be punished but I must have the truth. Tomorrow is Sunday. You shall go to church, and up to the minister you shall march, and he will ask you what I am asking you now. In the face of God you shall say to him that you did not take that apple, then I shall know. Did you or did you not take that apple? I will have the truth. And you my young sir, I shall not punish you but I must have the truth. You shall stay in bed all day tomorrow, all next week as long as it takes for one of you to change your story. I will have the truth.

The mountains are savage about the valley. The lake is bitter, scalding with the salt. They knew they had found the Dead Sea. At last the child confessed, with bitter and hard tears that he had taken the fruit himself. It was the truth.

Clear and cold the moon shone in the partly denuded poplars. It was midnight and the little fellow to whom he had determined to teach the meaning of the truth was snug in his bed. Years before that Utah had been admitted to the Union as a state and polygamy had been more or less abandoned. The young folk were beginning to be ashamed of the narrowness of their cult and the bones of the fathers were rotten.

The glassy half moon in the dark leaves cast a dull light over the world upon which a calm had descended. Suddenly the pleiades could be heard talking together in Phœnician. Their words were clear as dropping water : What things they do in this new world : they said. Let us from now on swear to each other that we will give up every thought of wisdom and seek no further for the truth — which is, after all a veritable moon. — At this the moon was overcast for a moment by a falling leaf. The answer that came from that clear but broken ball rose slowly toward the stars : The child is asleep. Let us warn him of the folly of words. Let us bless him only with words that change often and never stiffen nor remain to form sentences of seven parts. To him I send a message of words like running water.— At this the stars smiled for they were married to one —

Elena, yo soy un wonder, she would say. *Vu par le jury.* And who is the jury but myself. The boy had struck her with a stone. Come we shall go and apologise, said Brigham Young. Into the neighbour's kitchen they walked. An older sister was cleaning the gas range. Where is your sister ? But the truth is that all the while he had been hoping that just what had happened would happen. His eye ran up and down the girl's form. Secretly he was happy to have found her alone. I'm sorry, I will never do it again, Never again. Never again. Oh never, never again.

And how can I, now that it is all over, and I am old ? But at first I tell you I cried my eyes out. I had just been admitted to the Beaux Arts. All was as near perfect as could well be. I had the friendship of La Baronne d'Orsay and then the stars withdrew their aid. I had to go back to Porto Rico. I had to leave everything behind to go back to that country where there was nothing.

There life ended. But it is over now. I was just beginning to do things. I tell you I cried my eyes out. But I am old now. I wanted you to see these drawings, to show you it was not a bluff.

The Indians are gone. It is late now. It is cold. September is over. October is cold. Words should be — Words should be — I am tired to death.

But two enormous women, middle aged, dignified, with still broad backs came down the street just as the very dirty little boy was crossing over. The three arrived at the entrance to the path at the same moment. The women looked hard at the filthy little boy whose face was stickly from apple-juice and black, with a great circle of dirt around the mouth. The women looked and the little boy hung his head and stumbled off into the long grass, almost falling into the abandoned foundation.

And so the little company went on foot 20,000 miles along what later became known as Emigration Trail, overcoming incredible obstacles, eating the draught oxen, through savage mountains on, on to the Mountain Meadow Massacre. For they would worship the Lord their God in peace and in their own way. At last the Mayflower was in the harbor and the pilgrims had landed and dispersed.

Yes, it was a New World.

But they have prospered and today the Mormon Church is all for goodness and it is powerful and rich.

A favorite trick of the Mayo Indians is, if they meet a man with good clothes, to take what they want and let him go on in his drawers.

So it was with infinite satisfaction that on looking up the little boy saw those two terrible viragos suddenly as low as he. *Nuevo Mundo.*

CHAPTER IX.

ALANG-GLANG! Calang-glang! went the bells of the little Episcopal Church at Allandale. It was eight o'clock in the evening. A row of cars stood along the curb, each with its headlights lit, but dimmed so as not to make too much of a glare on the road, at the same time to save the battery while complying with the law!

On sped the little family all crowded into one seat, the two children sleeping.

In the Dutch church on the old Paramus Road Aaron Burr was married to Mrs. Prevost, Jataqua! It is near Hohokus, cleft-in-the-rocks, where the Leni Lenapes of the Delaware nation had their village from time immemorial. Aaron, my darling, life begins anew! It is a new start. Let us look forward staunchly together —

The long, palm-like leaves of the ailantus trees moved slowly up and down in the little wind, up and down.

And along this road came the British. Aaron, the youth from Princeton, gathered his command together and drove them back. Mother I cannot sleep in this bed, it is full of *British soldiers*. Why so it is! How horrid.

And he too, on his memorable retreat, that excellent judge of horseflesh, George Washington, he too had passed over this road ; and these trees, the oldest of them, had witnessed him. And now the wind has torn the finest of them in half.

Nothing more wonderful than to see the pears attached by their stems to the trees. Earth, trunk, branch, twig and the fruit : a circle soon to be completed when the pear falls. They had left at eleven and soon they would be home. The little car purred pleasantly to itself at the thought of the long night. Oh, to be a woman, thought the speeding mechanism. For they had wrapped something or other in a piece of newspaper and placed it under the seat and there were pictures there of girls — or grown women it might be, in very short skirts Steadily the wheels spun while on the paper were printed these words :

The Perfection of Pisek-designed Personality Modes : A distinctly forward move in the realm of fashion is suggested by the new personality modes, designed by Pisek... modes that are genuine inspirations of individual styling, created for meeting the personal preferences of a fastidiously fashionable clientèle, the woman and the miss who seek personality in dress in keeping with their charms, characteristics and station . . . Thus you can expect at Pisek's only those *tailleurs*, gowns, wraps and frocks that bear the unmistakable stamp of individuality — styles that encourage and inspire admiration for their splended simplicity and differentness... come to Pisek's . . . (the more the better) . . . see the new ideas in fashions . . . You'll not be disappointed . .

What chit of a girl could have appreciated you, my darling boy, as I do. A man of your personality, so fresh in wit, so brimming with vigor and new ideas. Aaron my dear, dear boy, life has not yet begun. All is new and untouched in the world waiting, like the pear on the tree, for you to pluck it. Everyone loves you and will wait on you. For you everything is possible. Bing! and Hamilton lies dead.

As old Mr. Goss, who lost his hearing from an explosion of fireworks in Philadelphia after Lee's defeat, has said in his high nasal twang : Quite right, quite right, I've seen the country saved 8 times in the last fifty years.

At any rate it was a new world to them ; they two together would conquer and use, life had smiled upon them. *Nuevo Mundo.*

Along the road the Dutch settlers came out from their attractive brown stone houses as the happy and distinguished couple went by. It was a great day for the little colony of New Jersey. There over the misty meadows the lights of Weehawken were beginning to glimmer as the little car and its precious freight drew near the end of the journey. The pear fell to the earth and was eaten by the pigs.

I wonder if he'll recognise me in my Greenwich Village honkie-tonk bobbed hair. The hairdresser said : Don't you do it, when I said I'd like mine bobbed too. So many of the girls had theirs done a year ago and now its just at that impossible stage where you can't do a thing with it. Better go to Europe or California until it grows again. There's a reason for travel : As the hair progresses the days grow fewer.

But is South Africa after all the country of the future?

Over the great spaces of New Jersey, Pennsylvania, Ohio, Indiana he sped in the Pullman car. .City after city swept up to him, paused awhile at his elbow and plunged away to the rear with the motion of a wheel whose hub was hidden in infinity. And such indeed was exactly the case. He was being ground between two wheels, one on either side of the car and it was their turning that thrust him forward at such speed. The wheat was up in the fields but a fellow passenger assured him that in Kansas, only two days before, he had seen wheat twice as high — which explains the cause of so many abandoned farms in Vermont, he remembered, and settled back to another hour of idle staring. A new country he kept saying to himself. On a siding were cars loaded with emigrants from Holland booked through to San Francisco.

Into the elevator stepped the young man in a petty officer's uniform. His Spanish was exquisite to hear. The first battleship since the Spanish-American war was anchored in New York harbor. How well he bears himself. The Spanish are the only people in Europe whom civilization has not ruined. Savage men, big bearded chins — but shaved clean. They know how to treat their women — better than the French for the French — after all are *blagueurs* to a man. The Spanish stand still. What an ass a man will make of himself in a strange country! In armor De Soto wandering haphazard over Alabama. The Seminoles for guides. Buried him in the Mississippi. It is my river, he said. Roll Jordan roll. It is *my* river for I discovered it and into it let my body, in full armor, be put to rest. The cat-fish ate it. So roll Jordan roll. Diada Daughter of Discord : read it.

In Illinois, far in the west, over that trackless waste of forest and mountain and river and lake they came at last to a valley that pleased them and there they determined to build. So they fell to hewing trees and building their houses, work to which they had been bred and trained for two generations since Plymouth and Salem days. Cornwallis had been beaten fifty years before

[43]

and Pitt had rushed to see the King crying : All is lost. A new world had been born. Here in the primeval forest the little colony of New Englanders hoped to realise success and plenty.

In Bonnie, Illinois, the Presbyterian minister is a very good man. He is as good a preacher as Bonnie can afford and if anybody said that Bonnie is made up of mad-men — He would be shot. *Nuevo Mundo*, shouted the sailors. But their cry was by now almost extinct.

In polite stories the world had been made acquainted with the picturesque lives of these commonplace but worthy people. In detail their story had been told. Over the precipice in Yosemite the Bridal Veil Falls had been launching its water for a thousand years and ignorance was fattening his belly apace.

Bonnie, Ill., October 22. Dear Bill : Am up to my ears in painting, and am preparing to go to Alton, Ill., to work in the State Hospital, if I get a call, so am too busy now to read your book but think I'm going to like it and will devour it later. Sincerely. A. N. Turner.

And the little boy crept into the great chest like Peppo into the Cardinal's tomb and began to pick up the mothballs that had been left there when the winter things were removed.

An Indian would sense the facts as he wished. A tree would speak to him with a definite identity. It would not at least seem endowed with human characteristics : a voice, that would be all.

CHAPTER X.

RNOLD, this wind is, the wise and sagacious captain. Henchman of the wind. The wind is a lion with hooked teeth. The saber-toothed tiger inhabited the region west of the Alleganies throughout the pleistocene age. With a snarl it wrenches the limbs of the trees from their places and tosses them to earth where they lie with the leaves still fluttering.

Vacuous ; full of wind. Her whole pelvis is full of intestine but aside from the ptosis I find nothing really wrong. The uterus appears to be normal. The bleeding may come from a cyst. At least there is no good reason for removing — for a hysterectomy. There it is. It. Like some tropical fruit color of the skunk cabbage flower. There it is, that mystical pear, glistening with the peritoneum. Here the cavern of all caverns. Alpha if not omega. Talk politely and obey the law. But do not remove it.

Oh my country. Shall it be a hysterectomy? Arnold there is a wind with a knife's edge.

And Remy says the spring of curiosity is broken at thirty. Nothing left at fifty but the facts of bed and table. He has the lilt of Heine at his best and in places quite equals the work of the author of Danny Deever. The catgut had slipped out of the needle. The young interne held the point of the suture between his fingers and the nurse approached the needle as accurately as she could. But the man's hand trembled slightly. For a moment they tried to complete the connection but failing in their attempt the nurse took the end in her other hand and soon had the needle threaded. The young doctor looked up as much as to say thank you.

Such a wind. At fifteen they seem noble, desirable beyond dreams. In the winter the trees at least remain stems of wood that resist with a will, whose branches rebound against the impact of sleet. At thirty they are what they are. The boy rebels and she with her hair in distressed tangles about the

[45]

disorderly boudoir cap, at mid-day, whines and snatches at him as he jerks and defies her. It is beyond her strength to control a boy of nine. Clutching her dressing sack — oh slobbery morsel — about her breastless form with one hand she rushes as far as she dares to the porch edge, glancing furtively about for chance gentlemen or neighbors and tries to overtake the youngster. No, the young man has really escaped. He goes to school filthy again and what will they think of his mother.

At fifteen they are slender and coquettish and they cry if you are rough with them. Great burly fellow, she seemed to him all that he was not, the quintessence of Ibsenism, the wind among the reeds. Or perhaps the reed in the wind. Something to love, to take into the arms, to protect — If you can find any reason for doing a hysterectomy doctor, do it. Her husband is good for nothing at all. She at least is a power in her family. She is not like the native American women of her class, she is a Polock. You never saw such courage.

The schooner left Southampton bound for New York with a cargo of rails — steel rails. But the English emigrants were not like these modern messes. Those round, expressionless peasant faces of today. See that one there with the little boy at her side. Castle Garden. At last we are to be in America, where gold is in the streets. Look at that face. That is the kind of immigration we want. Look at the power in that jaw. Look at that nose. She is one who will give two for every stroke she has to take. Look at the intensity of her gaze. Well, she's English, that's the reason. Nowadays they have no more of that sort. These Jews and Polocks, Sicilians and Greeks. Good-bye America!

The head nurse's legs under her practical short skirt were like mighty columns. They held the seriousness of her looks, her steady, able hands. A fine woman.

CHAPTER XI.

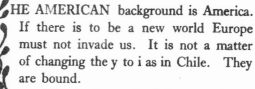HE AMERICAN background is America. If there is to be a new world Europe must not invade us. It is not a matter of changing the y to i as in Chile. They are bound.

The background of America is not Europe but America.

Eh bien mon vieux coco, this stuff that you have been writing today, do you mean that you are attempting to set down the American background? You will go mad. Why? Because you are trying to do nothing at all. The American background? It is Europe. It can be nothing else. Your very method proves what I say. You have no notion what you are going to write from one word to the other. It is madness. You call this the background of American life? Madness?

As far as I have gone it is accurate.

It is painting the wind.

Ah, that would be something.

Mais ça, are you a plain imbecile? That is a game for children. Why do you not do as so many of your good writers do? Your Edgar Lee Masters, your Winesburg, Ohio. Have you not seen the photographs of men and women on your walls? They are a type, as distinct as a Frenchman or a German. Study these men, know their lives. You have a real work to do, you have the talent, the opportunity even. This is your work in life. You Americans, you are wasteful, mad —

Our background.

You would paint the wind. Well, it has been tried — many times, and do you know where that leads?

I know where it has led.

But do you know? Have you seen, felt, heard what they have seen, felt, heard, our Villons —

Apollo was out of breath but the nymph was more tired than he. The chase must soon have ended when she falling to her knees half from the will to be there half from fatigue besought her mistress Diana to save her from the God's desire. And she was changed into a laurel bush.

All about the hills where they stood the hard waxen leaves of the laurel glistened above the dead leaves of the hardwood trees, the beech, the maple, the oak.

You imagine I am French because I attack you from the continental viewpoint. You are wrong. I am from the country of your friends Moussorgsky, Dostoiefsky, Chekov. At least if you will not yield me the point that America cannot be new, cannot do anything unless she takes the great heritage which men of all nations and ages have left to the human race.

You mean that I should not be an American but — Turgenef, enjoy you more if, well, if you were more comprehensible, a little more particular, *vous comprenez*? You sweep out your arms, you — I see no faces, no details of the life, no new shape —

The druggist's boy cannot be distinguished from his master when he says, Hello, over the phone — Is that what you mean?

Well, you are very much children, you Americans.

It is not to be avoided as far as I can see.

Let us have now a beginning of composition. We have had enough of your improvisations.

I am consumed by my lusts. No American can imagine the hunger I have.

It is the itch, monsieur. It is neurasthenia. Desire is not a thing to speak of as if it were a matter of filling the stomach. It is wind, gas. You are empty my friend. Eat. Then and then only.

Like all men save perhaps the Chinese you are most transparent when you imagine yourself most protected.

Her bosom reached almost to her knees. That morning in the October garden she had picked a violet for him and placed it in his coat. Watching the feet of men and women as they touched the pavement a strong odor of violets crossed his path.

He turned and saw the massive Jewess waddling by. It had been good perfume too.

These Polocks. Their heads have no occiput. They are flat behind. It is why when they put on their American hats the things slip down about their ears. The nigger's head isn't that way. You know how the bump goes out behind in so many of them. The club sandwich on her plate kept sliding apart, the top slice of bread would slip. Then she took the pieces in her fingers and poked the lettuce in under the sheet. On her breast was a black pin. It formed a circle. She looked up with her mouth full of food and resting both elbows on the table chewed America thoughtfully while she held the state of Maryland in her firm fingers. The ends of each finger were stubby, the nails cut short and as clean as well manicured nails could well be. Clatter, clatter, clatter. He could see himself in the plate glass behind her. He was conscious of his hat which he had not removed. He was at this table with these five women — one of them young, ready — and he had not removed his hat. There was in fact no place to put it.

I am begging, frankly. Ten cents a ticket. I have to raise fifty dollars by the end of next week. We want to fit up a room in our hall where the colored working girls can come and rest. On Thursdays we serve tea. Then they go back to the office. When the impact is over the man must think. I tell you I do not contemplate with relish seeing my children bred out of all these girls. Is it wrong? Well, I thought you said you had an appetite. Impregnate eighty of them, right and left as you see them here in this room. It would not be impossible. I cannot think of my children running about in the environment in which these have to live. My dear sir, you are a fool. You are lying to yourself — As to the girls, I frankly desire them. I desire many, many, many.

There she sat on the bench of the subway car looking idly about, being rushed under the river at great speed to the kitchen of her mother's flat. Malodorous mother. Or wrinkled hard-put-to-it mother. Savior of the movies. After the impact his great heart had expanded so as to include the whole city, every woman young and old there he having impregnated with sons and daughters. For everyone loved him. And he knew how to look into their eyes with both passion and understanding. Each had taken him to her soul of souls where the walls were papered with editorials from the Journal and there he had made himself father to her future child. As they went upstairs he saw how her heels were worn — Who will understand the hugeness of my passion?

But he had understood. The truth lay under the surface. Why then not — No two can remain together without training. Who better than that one who is practiced. The faithful husband of the clothing store madam is used to her. They functionate well together. He puts his hat in the right place. His money in the right bank. His arm fitted in just the posture best suited to their mutual height and width. All their practices were mated.

But he was an outsider. He was new to all. Her shoes are stitched up the back.

Card-index minds, the judges have. Socialism, immorality and lunacy are about synonyms to the judge. Property is sacred and human liberty is bitter, bitter, bitter to their tongues.

Walk up the stairs there little girl. But she is naked! These are all doctors. So the little tot struggled up the very high clinic steps, naked as she was, and all the doctors looked at her. She had some spots on her body that had been there a year. Had I been her father I would know why I am a fool.

Naked and free, free to be damned in to hell by a chance vagrant to whom she had taken a fancy. Her father did not know her. Did not even know that she existed. Cared less. We will look after her said the head doctor.

CHAPTER XII.

HAT cat is funny. I think she'd be a good one for the circus. When she's hungry she bites your legs. Then she jumps at you as much as to say : *Carramba*, give me something.

America needs the flamboyant to save her soul — said Vachel Lindsay to the indifferent mountains.

He might have added that America tries to satisfy this need in strange and often uncatalogued ways. America, living an exemplary three-meals-a-day-and-bed-time life in a wall-papered home, goes now and then *en masse*, by Gosh, to the circus to see men, women and animals perform exquisite and impossible feats or daring. What could be more flamboyant than the trapeze-performer hurtling through the air, the tiger leaping through man-made hoops, or the elephant poising his mighty bulk on his two forelegs lifted to the top of bottles? What more flamboyant than the painted clown, timeless type of the race, laughing that he may not weep, grinning through a thousand tragic jests while little human beings perform their miraculous tricks around him?

Jazz, the Follies, the flapper in orange and green gown and war-paint of rouge — impossible frenzies of color in a world that refuses to be drab. Even the movies, devoid as they are of color in the physical sense, are gaudy in the imaginations of the people who watch them ; gaudy with exaggerated romance, exaggerated comedy, exaggerated splendor or grotesqueness or passion. Human souls who are not living impassioned lives, not creating romance and splendor and grotesqueness — phases of beauty's infinite variety — such people wistfully try to find these things outside themselves ; a futile, often a destructive quest.

The imagination will not down. If it is not a dance, a song, it becomes an outcry, a protest. If it is not flamboyance it becomes deformity ; if it is not art, it becomes crime. Men and women cannot be content, any more than children, with the mere

[51]

facts of a humdrum life — the imagination must adorn and exaggerate life, must give it splendor and grotesqueness, beauty and infinite depth. And the mere acceptance of these things from without is not enough — it is not enough to agree and assert when the imagination demands for satisfaction creative energy. Flamboyance expresses faith in that energy — it is a shout of delight, a declaration of richness. It is at least the beginning of art.

All right go ahead : A TEXAS PRIZE CONTEST — The Southern Methodist University at Dallas, Texas, recently emerged from a prize contest which had a strange *dénouement* —

Look here young man, after this you examine those girls in the cold weather.

Who is Warner Fabian? *Flaming Youth* is the story of the super-flapper, of her affairs at country clubs and cozy home-dances with all the accompaniments of prohibition stimulants. Warner Fabian believes that the youth of this country feeds on excitement and rushes to knowledge "heeled" by way of petting parties and the elemental stimulus of jazz. The barriers of convention are down. Youth makes its own standards and innocence, according to the author, has been superseded by omniscience.

It doesn't matter that Warner Fabian is a *nom de plume* which conceals the identity of one of the ablest scientists of this country who has dared to look facts in the face, facts physical, moral and emotional. He has written the truth about youth, the youth of today as he sees it.

FLAMING YOUTH by Warner Fabian is the writing on the wall. It is the *Quo Vadis* of the present moment.

Those who are following in the Metropolitan Magazine the fortunes of Pat, the most sophisticated and yet at the same time one of the most deliciously lovely heroines of recent novels, and the fortunes of her two sisters, may protest that Mr. Fabian's portrayal of youth in this novel is outscotting Fitzgerald and overdancing in the Dark. We feel however that this story of three girls and their many men is one which may sufficiently frighten mothers and electrify fathers and hit the younger set hard enough between the eyes to help America's youth to, at least, a gradual return to sanity.

And so the beginning of art ends in a gradual return to sanity.

To-day Modern scientific research has provided the most efficient agent for the treatment of local inflamation : DIONAL applied locally over the affected area acts promptly with prolonged effect. Drugless. Non-irritant. Non-toxic. Indicated in Mastitis, Burns, Boil, Tonsilitis, Mastoiditis, Sprain, Abcess, Bronchitis, Mumps, Contusion, Ulcers, Pneumonia.

If a man died on a stretcher he simply said : Dump it out. And ordered us back for another load.

Intended to stop at the school but his mind waylaid him. Down the hill came the ash-cart — on the wrong side of the street. He, up the hill, perforce went wrong also and with great headway. Just as he was about to pass the cart another car swung out from behind it, headed down hill at full speed. It was too late for any of the three to stop. In three seconds there would be death for someone. Angels would be waiting for mother's little boy. Without the minutest loss of time, in time with the Boston Symphony Orchestra at its best he swung far to the left, up over the curb, between two trees, onto the sidewalk — by luck no one was passing — and going fifty feet came back between two trees, over the curb to the roadway and continued his empty progress, rather hot in the face, it must be confessed. He felt happy and proud.

. But he had missed his street.

Well let it go. Far away in front of him a locomotive stood indifferently at the avenue end, emitting great clouds of smoke. It was autumn, clear and cold.

But you Scandinavians, said the Frenchman, it is impossible to live in this way. Why France, which is ten times as rich as your countries, could not do it. You do not know what money is for. You throw it away like a sickness. To drink champagne like this is madness, and it is every night, everywhere, in Christiania, Copenhagen, everywhere.

And there she sits staring out, not at the sea, but over Long Island Sound. Dreaming of her sons — and of the money she will make next year by renting the better of her two little shacks.

When you have paid up the twenty shares you may, if you like, retain them as paid up shares in which case you will receive the 5 % interest, or, if you feel that you would like to do so, you may increase your holding to thirty shares and receive the 6 %. Of course everyone is not able to do that. Do not worry about it, we will notify you in plenty of time when your book is balanced at the end of the six months.

Let's see. What is the number of your house? Four eighty? I'll see that they send it right up.

You know last Sunday was my birthday. Seventy-three years old. I had a party, a surprise party — my relatives came from all sides. But I couldn't get her downstairs. She's afraid. We had a banister put on the stairs, cost me nine dollars but she will not do it. She's so fat you know, she's afraid of falling.

Re Commissions due — Amount $1.00. Dear Sir : — You will please take notice that unless we receive payment in full of your account within FIVE DAYS after receipt of this letter, we shall draw upon you for the amount due.

A collection agency draft notifies the banks — those great institutions of finance — that there is serious doubt regarding the way you pay your honest obligations. The bank will take note of it. From there the information quietly passes to the various Mercantile Agencies, Dun's, Bradstreet's, Martindale's. And this is ONLY ONE cog in the wheel of ARROW SERVICE. Our reports cover the whole field of credit reporting.

Your continued indifference to our requests for payment has forced us to consider this action. The draft, with a full history of the debt leaves our office in five days unless your check is received in the meantime.

Let your better judgement guide you, and pay this account without any more trouble or expense. Yours very truly — MEMBERS : Retail Credit Men's National Association. Commercial Law League of America. Rotary International. O Rotary International!

At this, De Soto, sick, after all the months of travel, stopped out of breath and looked about him. Hundreds of miles he had travelled through morass after morass, where the trees were so thick that one could scarcely get between them, over mountain and river but never did he come to the other side. The best he had done was to locate a river running across his path, the greatest he had ever seen or heard of, greater than the Nile,

greater than the Euphrates, no less indeed than any. Here he
had confronted the New World in all its mighty significance and
something had penetrated his soul so that in the hour of need
he had turned to this Mighty River rather than to any other
thing. Should it come to the worst he had decided what to do.
Out of the tangle around him, out of the mess of his own past
the river alone could give him rest. Should he die his body
should be given to this last resting place. Into it Europe should
pass as into a new world.

Near the shore he saw a school of small fish which seemed
to look at him, rippling the water as they moved out in unison.
Raising his heavy head De Soto gave the order to proceed. Four
of the men lifted him on an improvised stretcher and the party,
headed by the Indians, started again north along the bank.

The whole country was strange to them. But there at
the edge of that mighty river he had seen those little fish who
would soon be eating him, he, De Soto the mighty explorer —
He smiled quietly to himself with a curious satisfaction.

CHAPTER XIII.

T WAS a shock to discover that she, that most well built girl, so discrete, so comely, so able a thing in appearance, should be so stupid. There are things that she cannot learn. She will never finish school. Positively stupid. Why her little brother, no bigger than Hop o' my Thumb has caught up to her and will soon outstrip her. Her older brother is the brightest boy in the High School. She will I suppose breed stupid children. Plant wizards choose the best out of lots running into the millions. Choose here there everywhere for hybrids. A ten-pound white leghorn cockerel, hens that lay eggs big enough to spoil the career of any actor. She might though have bright children. What a pity that one so likely should be so stupid. Easier to work with but I should hate a child of mine to be that way. Excuses — Try first. Argue after. Excuses. Do not dare.

There sat the seven boys — nine years old and there-abouts — planning dire tortures for any that should seduce or touch in any way their sisters. Each strove to exceed the other. Tying his antagonist to a tree Apollo took out his knife and flayed him. For sweet as the flute had been yet no man can play the flute and sing at the same time. But the God had first played his harp and then sung to his own accompaniment — a thing manifestly unfair. No doubt, his sense of being in the wrong whetted his lust for the other's hide. In any case he got what he was after. He was the winner and that was all there was about it.

Each boy would think with a secret glow of a new torture : I would dip his hands in boiling lead — they often melted old pieces of lead in a plumber's pot over a field fire to make slugs for their bean shooters — then I would tie a rope to his feet and drag him on cinders etc.... each inventing a worse torture than that pictured before. And all for their sisters' virtue. So there under the east wall of the Episcopal Church they sat in a group on the grass and talked together for an hour.

The real empire builders of our colonial period were not the statesmen, the men of wealth, the great planters but the unknown pioneers who fought single-handed and at once both the primeval wilderness and the lurking savage. The hand crooked to the ploughtail was shaped to the trigger.

The Mesa Verde cliff dwellers — a much advanced race — formed a partnership with nature in the science of home building. Masterpieces of architecture; the survivals of the cliff dwellings tell the story of the ages.

On the top of a point high above the steep cliffs stood Sun Temple, so called, scene of the great ceremonial dramas of the clan. The building is in the form of the letter D and many of the stones which make up the thousand-odd feet of walls are highly decorated.

The corner stone of the building contains a fossil leaf of a palm tree. Influenced by anything which even in shape resembled the sun, the primitive people walled in the leaf on three sides and made a shrine.

The word *bayeta* is merely Spanish for *baize*. Great quantities of this were made in England for the Spanish and Mexican trade, the major part of which was of a brilliant red color. In this way English *baize* became Spanish *bayeta* to the Indians of the American Southwest. Familiar with the art of weaving, these Indians unraveled the bayeta, retwisted it into one, two or three strands, and then rewove it into their blankets, which are now almost priceless. This old blanket was picked up by the author in a New Mexican corral, for the purpose of wiping his buggy axle. It was covered with filth and mud. A number of washings revealed this glorious specimen of the weaver's art.

Accepted by a cultured and talented belle, Lincoln, according to his law partner, had already been refused by Sarah Rickard, an obscur miss of sixteen, of whom apparently nothing further is known.

It was twelve feet from the rock into the water. As he stood looking down it seemed twenty. His eyes being five feet from his heels made it seem by that much higher than it was. He had never dived from such a height in his life. He had climbed up there to dive and he must dive or yield. What would he yield? At least it was something he did not intend to yield. He tried his best to imitate the others, he stood on the edge and plunged.

It seemed to him that he plunged. As a matter of fact he dropped over the edge with his body bent almost double so that his thighs hit the water with a stinging impact, also the lower part of his belly, also the top of his head. He did not feel certain of himself for a moment or two after rising to the surface. That was about enough. Memory began to fill the blank of his mind.

There it was still, the men around Mrs. Chain's table on Locust St.: $3.50 a week. A week? Yes, three-fifty a week. And that place in Leipzig where they had only half cooked fresh pork. *Schwein schlacherei*! Bah. One week was enough there. Fraulein Dachs, *pflaumen suppe*. That purple and sweet soup. The white cakes they sold on the station platform near Malaga, what were they called? It seemed to be some native bake peculiar to the place. The devil fish in a black sauce in Seville. Big lumps of dough, big as snowballs, *sauer braten*. But Mrs. Chain's prunes were the most wonderful. Watery tidbits. It was prunes or applesauce. Her daughter was simple I guess. Did her best to land one of the students, kept it up for twenty years. At that table I met one of my dearest friends. Will you have some bread? Yes. That look. It was enough. Youth is so rich. It needs no stage setting. Out went my heart to that face. There was something soft there, a reticence, a welcome, a loneliness that called to me. And he, he must have seen it in me too. We looked, two young men, and at once the tie was cemented. It was gaged accurately at once and sealed for all time. The other faces are so many prunes.

Have you ever seen a dish of small birds all lying on their backs on the dish and with feet in the air, all roasted stiff but brown and savory? Rice birds I think they called them. Or snails or baked eggs?

The old man raked slowly. It took him all day to finish the small lawn. But it was autumn and the leaves had fallen thickly. The bird bath was full of leaves. It was a sentimental picture. But after all why? The leaves must fall into every corner. If they fall into the bird bath that is all there is to it. Still it calls many things to the mind that are not evoked by the twingling of waves on a lake shore in August.

Clark had taken a job as clerk at Pocono, and she was a Quakeress. They got to know each other very, very well. And this girl in the steamer chair, it was the cattle men who attracted her. Let her go then, he said tying the cord with a piece of gauze twisted into a rope. When you bathe the baby for the first time do not put him into a tub but sponge him off carefully before the fire with castile soap and warm water. Be careful not to get the soap into his eyes. Is it nitrate of silver they use for a baby's eyes?

I could not tell whether it was a baby or a doll the little girl was coddling. The Italians' babies are often so very small. They dress them up so grotesquely too. It must be a rigid custom with them.

Nothing at all. All at once it seemed that every ill word he had ever heard spoken struck his ear at the same moment. What a horrible roar it made. But there were other things, too many to record. Corners of rooms sacred to so many deeds. Here he had said so and so, done so and so. On that picnic he had dared to be happy. All the older women had watched him. With one girl under each arm he had let his spirit go. They had been closer than anything he could now imagine.

CHAPTER XIV.

ARTICLES of falling stars, coming to nothing. The air pits them, eating out the softer parts. Sometimes one strikes the earth or falls flaming into Lake Michigan with a great hiss and roar. And if the lawless mob that rules Ireland with its orderly courts and still more orderly minds will not desist it must be crushed by England. So that to realize the futility of American men intent upon that virtue to be found in literature, literature, that is, of the traditional sort as known in France and Prussia — to realize how each serious American writer in turn flares up for a moment and fizzles out, burnt out by the air leaving no literary monument, no Arc de Triomphe behind him, no India subdued — To realize this it is necessary to go back to the T'ang dynasty where responsibility rested solely on the heads of the poets — etc.. etc... Or better still why not seek in Aleppo or Jerusalem for the strain to save us.

America is lost. Ah Christ, Ah Christ that night should come so soon.

And the reason is that no American poet, no American man of letters has taken the responsibility upon his own person. The responsibility for what? There is the fire. Rush into it. What is literature anyway but suffering recorded in palpitating syllables? It is the quiet after the attack. Picking a sliver of bone from his mangled and severed leg he dipped it in his own gore and wrote an immortal lyric. Richard Cœur de Lion shot through the chest with an iron bolt wrote the first English — no, French, poem of importance. What of democratic Chaucer? He was only a poet but Richard was a man, an adventurer, a king. The half mad women rush to impregnate themselves against him. And this is literature. This is the great desirable. Soaked in passion, *baba au rhum*, the sheer proof of the spirit will do the trick and America will be King. Up America. Up Cœur de Lion. Up Countess Wynienski the queen of Ireland.

Polyphemus took first one shape then another but Odysseus, the wise and crafty, held firm. He did not let go but Polyphemus did. In fact the God could not exist without Odysseus to oppose him.

Why man, Europe is YEARNING to see something new come out of America.

In a soup of passion they would see a little clam. Let us smile. This is —

The danger is in forgetting that the good of the past is the same good of the present. That the power that lived then lives today. That we too possess it. That true novelty is in good work and that no matter how good work comes it is good when it possesses power over itself. Europe's enemy is the past. Our enemy is Europe, a thing unrelated to us in any way. Our lie that we must fight to the last breathe is that it is related to us.

We are deceived when they cry that negro music is the only true American creation. It IS the only true from the European point of view. Everything is judged from that point of view. But to us it is only new when we consider it from a traditional vantage. To us it means a thousand things it can never mean to a European. To us only can it be said to be alive. With us it integrates with our lives. That is what it teaches us. What in hell does it matter to us whether it is new or not when it IS to us. It exists. It is good solely because it is a part of us. It is good THEREFORE and therefore only is it new. Everything that is done in Europe is a repetition of the past with a difference. Everything we do must be a repetition of the past with a difference. I mean that if negro music is new in an absolute sense — which it is not by any means, if we are to consider the Ethiopian — the probable Ethiopian influence in Egypt — then it is new to Europe as it is to us.

It is not necessary for us to learn from anyone but ourselves — at least it would be a relief to discover a critic who looked at American work from the American viewpoint.

We are a young nation and have not had time or opportunity to catch up with nations that had ten centuries start of us. We still labor under the handicap of our Puritan lineage....

We shall not be able to plead childhood any longer.

Eric the Red landed in Providence, Long Island, and was put in a cage so everyone could see him.

This sort of stupidity we have to combat. I am not talking of the mass of plumbers and carpenters. I am talking of the one thing that is permanent. Spirits. I am saying that America will screw whom it will screw and when and how it will screw. And that it will refrain from screwing when it will and that no amount of infiltration tactics from "superior civilizations" can possibly make us anything but bastards.

We are only children when we acknowledge ourselves to be children. Weight of culture, weight of learning, weight of everything such as abandon in any sense has nothing to do with it. We must first isolate ourselves. Free ourselves even more than we have. Let us learn the essentials of the American situation.

We who despise the blackguards in the old sense. We too are free. Free! We too, with paddles instead of turbines will discover the new world. We are able. We are kings in our own right.

We care nothing at all for the complacent Concordites? We can look at that imitative phase with its erudite Holmeses, Thoreaus, and Emersons. With one word we can damn it : England.

In Patagonia they kick up the skulls of the river men out of the dust after a flood. In Peru, in Michu Pichu the cyclopean wall on the top of the Andes remains to rival the pyramids which after all may have been built of blocks of some plaster stuff of which we have lost the combination.

I know not a land except ours that has not to some small extent made its title clear. Translate this into ancient Greek and offer it to Harvard engraved on copper to be hung in the waterclosets which freshmen use.

And why do they come to naught? these falling stars, etc.

It has been generally supposed that among the peoples of the earth the age of maturity comes earliest in the tropics and increases gradually as one goes northward. But in North America this rule has one striking exception. It is not rare among Esquimau women that they have their first child at 12 and children born before the mothers were 11 have been recorded. Point Barrow Alaska 300 miles north of the Arctic circle.

But the early maturity of the Esquimau girls is strictly in accord with the supposition that the hotter the environment the earlier the maturity. To all intents and purposes the typical Esquimau lives under tropical or subtropical conditions. The temperature of the Esquimau house indoors frequently rises to 90°. When they go out the cold air does not have a chance to come in contact with the body, except for the limited area of the face. When an Esquimau is well dressed his two layers of fur clothing imprison the body heat so effectively that the air in actual contact with his skin is always at the temperature of a tropical summer. He carries the climate about with him inside his clothes.

When an Esquimau comes inside such a house as the one I have been speaking of he strips off all clothing, immediately on entering, except his knee breeches, and sits naked from the waist up and from the knees down. Great streams of perspiration run down the face and body and are being continually mopped up with handfuls of moss.

The effect of the overheated houses is more direct upon the women than the men for they remain indoors a large part of the winter.

Otherwise in North America among the Indians as one goes north from Mexico toward the arctic sea the colder the average temperature of the air that is in contact with the body through the year, the later the maturity of the girls. The most northerly of the Atabasca Indians appear to suffer a great deal from the cold.

The Dog Rib and Yellow Knife Indians are often so poorly clad that they have to be continually moving, for if they stop for even half an hour at a time their hands become completely numb.

In the evenings their wigwams are cheerful with a roaring fire but while one's face is almost scorched with the heat of the roaring flames one's back has hoar-frost forming upon it. At night the Indians go to sleep under their blankets covering up their heads and shivering all night. The average age of maturity of the girls of these tribes is as high or higher than that of north European whites.

But north from the Slavey and Dog Rib Indians to the Esquimau country the conditions suddenly change. One comes in contact with a people that has a system of living almost perfectly adapted to a cold climate, while the northern Indians have a system almost unbelievably ill adapted to the conditions in which they live.

In Puritan New England they wrapped the lover and his lass in one blanket and left them before the dying hearth after the family retired. There was a name for it which I have forgotten.

CHAPTER XV.

I T WAS another day ended. Another day added to the days that had gone before. Merest superstition. The eternal moment remained twining in its hair the flowers of yesterday and tomorrow. The newer street lights sparked in the dark. The uphill street which that morning had been filled at its far end with the enormous medal-with-rays of the sun was now flecked with sparkles. It was Carlstadt, established as a free thinker's corporation by Carl Weiss of Berne from which all churches had been excluded. Another day — any day —.

There lay that great frame of a man with his heavy features relaxed his loose jowls rising and falling with each breath while the busy surgeons tinkered at his elbow. Soon they struck gold and out spurted the red. Martha, who had not gone downstairs for over an hour caught it in a white porcelain bowl, an ounce, two ounces — she thought — estimating the amount swiftly. Then four ouces, eight. He was a large man. When will they check it! His breathing had grown easier. He was benefitted. A pint! He was white. In an hour men on horseback were riding north and south. Washington was dead. It was another day. Any day.

Davy Crockett had a literary style. Rather than blow his squirrel to bits he'd strike the tree just under its belly so that the concussion would stun it. Such was the country with the element of time subtracted. What is time but an impertinence?

Homesteading in the far western states was a struggle. Every child born there had a mother who is thrice a heroine. A woman in such a country approached motherhood at a time when her lusband had to be away from home. Up to the day of her confinement she had to milk, churn, care for the chickens, work in the garden and carry water to the house from a well three hundred yards away... The day of her confinement she did a large washing then walked two miles to the home of a neighbor.

For that the brat seized her by the lug with his little sharp teeth and drew blood. We'll have to put him on the bottle.

Nothing, save for the moment! In the moment exists all the past and the future! Evolution —! Anti-peristalsis. Eighty-seven years ago I was born in a little village in the outskirts of Birmingham. The past is for those that lived in the past, the present is for today. Or — today! The little thing lay at the foot of the bed while the midwife — It was in England 1833. And now by the sea a new world death has come and left his chewing gum in an artery of her brain. But I'll pay you for this, she said as they were sliding her into the ambulance, I'll pay you for this. You young people think you are awfully smart, don't you. I don't want to see them again, those fuzzy things, what are they, trees?

Good gracious, do you call this making me comfortable? The two boys had her on the stretcher on the floor. Yes, stay here a week then I can do what I please but you want to do what you please first. I wonder how much she planned.

CHAPTER XVI.

NOTHER day, going evening foremost this time. Leaning above her baby in the carriage was Nettie Vogelman, grown heavier since we knew her in the sixth grade twenty-five years before and balancing great masses of prehistoric knowledge on her head in the shape of a purple ostrichplume hat.

But where is romance in all this — with the great-coat she was wearing hanging from the bulge of her paps to the sidewalk? Romance! When knighthood was in flower. Rome. Eliogabalus in a skirt married his man servant.

We struggle to comprehend an obscure evolution — opposed by the true and static church — when the compensatory involution so plainly marked escapes our notice. Living we fail to live but insist on impaling ourselves on fossil horns. But the church balanced like a glass ball where the jets of evolution and involution meet has always, in its prosperous periods, patronised the arts.

What else could it do ?   Religion is the shell of beauty.

The fad of evolution is swept aside. It was only mildly interesting at the best. I'll give you a dollar my son for each of these books you read : Descent of Man and Origin of Species, reprinted by Dombie and Sons, Noodle Lane, Ken. W. London. England 1890.

Who will write the natural history of involution beginning with the stone razor age in Cornwall to the stone razor age in Papua? Oh China, China teach us! Ottoman, Magyar, Moor, teach us. Norse Eric the Discoverer teach us. Cœur de Lion, teach us. Great Catherine teach us. Phryne, Thaïs, Cleopatra, Brunehilde, Lucretia Borgia teach us. What was it, Demosthenes, that she said to you ? Come again ?

Borne on the foamy crest of involution, like Venus on her wave, stript as she but of all consequence — since it is the return : See they return! From savages in quest of a bear we are come upon rifles, cannon. From Chaldeans solving the stars we have fallen into the bellies of the telescopes. From great runners we have evolved into speeches sent over a wire.

But our spirits, our spirits have prospered! Boom, boom. Oh yes, our spirits have grown —

The corrosive of pity, Baroja says, giving up medicine to be a baker.

Marriage is of the church because it is the intersection of *loci* by which alone there is place for a church to stand. Beauty is an arrow. Diana launched her shaft into the air and where the deer and the arrow met a church was founded and there beauty had died.

So youth and youth meet and die and there the church sets up its ceremony.

Who will write the natural history of involution?

I have forgotten something important that I wanted to say. Thus having forgotten and remembered that it was important the folly of all thought is revealed.

The deer lay panting on the leaves while Diana leaned over it to stab it in the neck with her dagger.

I have forgotten what I wanted to say.

Venus and Adonis.

The second time I saw her it was in a room of a hotel in the city.

CHAPTER XVII.

S THE Southern mountains are not like other mountains, so the mountaineers are not like others. For all their beauty these mountains are treacherous and alien, and the people who must wring a livelihood from the sawmills or from the tiny perpendicular farms high up under the sky come to be wary and secret like their woodlands.

The Cumberland mountain mother, by nature sharp and sane, has studied the moods of the mountains and of the animals. Illiterate though she be, she is full of ripe wisdom. Many, superior to the mountain woman in, say, sanitation might learn from sitting on cabin doorsteps that they are most often inferior to her in sanity.

Yet, frankly, it is often better to sit on the cabin doorstep than to go inside. The mountain mother struggles bravely against dirt, but if you live in a lonely two-room cabin, if you are the sole caretaker of six children under ten, and two cows and a large stony garden, and must help in the cornfield besides, you are excusable if in the end you "quit struggling." The mountain mother does not make herself and her husband and her children slaves to the housekeeping arts.

A mountain woman dips snuff — surreptitiously if she is young, frankly if she is old.

We settle down on the doorstep probably on straight chairs with seats of cornhusks twisted into a rope and then interwoven. There is a sound to which the mountains have accustomed me — the sharp jolting thud when a mother, if she posesses neither cradle nor rocker, puts her baby to sleep by jerking forward and backward on two legs of a straight chair. There is usually some two-year-old lying fast asleep on the bed just inside the door ; or on the porch floor, plump and brown as a bun and studded with flies thick as currants.

Mountain children are as vigorous as baby oaks until they reach their 'teens, and then over-work begins to tell on growing bodies. A reedy boy of thirteen, just beginning to stretch to the length of spine and limb that characterises the mountaineer, often gets a stoop that he never afterward conquers. In the more remote lumber districts I have seen boys of ten and twelve work all day loading cars. There too, slim mountain girls of twelve and fourteen stand all day in the icy spray of the flume to stack bark on the cars.

Here where isolation makes people fiercely individualistic public opinion is as slow to deny a man's right to marry at the age he wishes as it is to deny his right to turn his corn into whisky. At the age when boys and girls first awake to the fact of sex they marry and the parents, although regretfully, let them.

The unmarried mother is most rare. A boy of sixteen sets himself to all the duties of fatherhood. A fourteen-year-old mother, with an ageless wisdom, enters without faltering on her future of a dozen children.

But here is Lory. But again a disgression — : In any account of the mountains one must remember that there are three distinct types : the people of the little villages, almost all remote from railroads ; the itinerant lumber workers, wood-choppers and mill-hands who follow the fortunes of the portable sawmill as it exhausts first one remote cove then another ; and the permanent farmers who have inherited their dwindling acres for generations. Yet at bottom the mountain mother is always the same.

Lory lives in a one-room lumber shack, and moves about once in three months. The walls are of planks with inch-wide cracks between them. There are two tiny windows with sliding wooden shutters and a door. All three must be closed when it is very cold. For better protection the walls are plastered over with newspapers, always peeling off and gnawed by woodrats. The plank floor does not prevent the red clay from oozing up. The shack is some fifteen feet square. It contains two stoves, two beds, two trunks, a table and two or three chairs. In it live six souls : two brothers, their wives and a baby apiece.

Lory is part Indian, one surmises from the straight hair dropping over her eyes and her slow squawlike movements. Her face is stolid except when it flashes into a smile of pure fun. Dark though she is her breast, bared from her dark purple dress, is statue white. She looks down on her first baby with a madonna's love and her words have in them a madonna's awe before a holy thing: "I ain't never a-goin' to whip him. He ain't never a-goin' to need it, for he won't get no meanness if I don't learn him none."

The setting is fairyland. Mountain folk go far toward living on beauty. The women may become too careless and inert even to scrape away the underbrush and plant a few sweet potatoes and cabbages. They may sit through lazy hours mumbling their snuff sticks, as does Mrs. Cole, while children and dogs and chickens swarm about them: but even Mrs. Cole can be roused by the call of beauty.

"My husband he's choppin' at the first clearin' two miles from here, and he's been plumb crazy over the yaller lady slippers up that-a-way. He's been sayin' I must take the two least kids, what ain't never seen sech, and go up there and see 'em 'fore they was gone. So yesterday we went. It sure was some climb over them old logs, but Gawd them lady slippers was worth it."

I shall never understand the mystery of a mountain woman's hair. No matter how old, how worn or ill she may be, her hair is always a wonder of color and abundance.

Ma Duncan at fifty-five is straight and sure-footed as an Indian; tall and slim and dark as a gypsy, with a gypsy's passionate love of out-of-doors. Her neighbors send for Ma Duncan from far and near in time of need. Going forth from her big farm boarding-house on errands of mercy. Up wild ravines to tiny cabins that seem to bud out like lichens from grey boulders wet with mountain streams, over foot logs that sway crazily over rock creeks, through waist-high undergrowth Ma Duncan goes with her stout stick.

As we reach a little grassy clearing Ma Duncan drops down to stretch out happily: So as I can hear what the old earth has to say me... Reckon it says, "Quit your fussin' you old fool. Ain't God kept your gang a young uns all straight so fur? He ain't a-going back on you now, just because they're growd."

Presently Ma Duncan sits up, her hands about her knees, her hat fallen from her wealth of hair, her gun on the ground beside her — often she carries a gun in the hope of getting a gray squirrel to be done in inimitable brown cream gravy for breakfast.

She looks out sadly over much worn woodland, with the great stumps remaining :

"I wish you could have seen the great old trees that used to be here. If folks wasn't so mad for money they might be here and a preachin' the gospel of beauty. But folks is all for money and all for self. Some-day when they've cut off all the beauty that God planted to point us to him, folks will look round and wonder what us human bein's is here fur —"

The mountain woman lives untouched by all modern life. In two centuries mountain people have changed so little that they are in many ways the typical Americans."

"The Lord sent me back" former pastor tells men in session at the church. With tears in his eyes, he enters meeting, escorted by two sons. Dramatic scene follows as he asks forgiveness for mistake he has made. Was in Canada and Buffalo. His explanation of absence is satisfactory to family and members he met last night.

Miss Hannen in seclusion at home. Her family declines to give statement.

Dominie Cornelius Densel, forty eight years old, former pastor, etc... who left his wife and eight children etc. came home last night.

Miss T. Hannen, twenty-six years old, etc... who disappeared from her home, etc... on the same afternoon that the dominie was numbered among the missing also came to her home the same evening.

Pictures of the missing dominie and member of his church who are home again.

CHAPTER XVIII.

OMMODIUS renamed the tenth month Amazonius. But he died a violent death and the old name was returned.

I had five cents in my pocket and a piece of apple pie in my hand, said Prof. M. I. Pupin, of Columbia University' describing the circumstances of his arrival in America in the steerage of the steamship Westphalie from Hamburg half a century ago.

Today that American scholar of Serbian birth holds the chair in electro-mechanics at Columbia University.

Prof. Pupin is merely one of a host of former immigrants whose names are linked with the great strides in science, commerce, finance and industry and whose careers furnish living proof that America, besides breeding great men, imports them.

Claude Monet was born in Columbia, Ohio.

In industry and commerce the stories of many of the successful immigrants read like romances.

There is C. C. A. Baldi of Philadelphia who began with nothing and who is now one of America's foremost citizens of foreign birth. When he landed in this country thirty years ago he had only a few pennies in the pockets of his ragged trowsers. He knew no English and knew nothing of American customs, but he had heard of the opportunities which America offers to a wide-awake, ambitious immigrant willing to work.

Mr. Baldi bought thirty lemons with his pennies. He peddled them and with the proceeds of sales bought more lemons and peddled them. Before long he had a cart loaded with hundreds of lemons. In time the push-cart became a store and the store grew into a great business.

Other spectacular instances of success are furnished by the careers of Louis J. Horowitz, one of America's greatest builders and S. M. Schatzkin, who came to this country twenty-five years ago with 3 dollars carefully tucked away in his clothes and began peddling coal in the East side of New York. To-day Schatzkin has large sums invested in many big American enterprises.

Horowitz, who came here thirty years ago, built the Woolworth and the Equitable buildings, one the tallest and the other the largest office building in point of floor space in the world. His first job was that of an errand boy. Later he worked as a parcel wrapper, then as a stock boy and then as a shoe salesman. After selling shoes he started selling real estate.

Witness, oh witness these lives my dainty cousins. Dear Madam : — It has often been said that one of the most interesting spots in America is the small space covered by the desk of the editor of the Atlantic Monthly.

All the qualities which make up the interest of life, — joy, sorrow, romance, ambition, experience, — seem to center in this spot in turn, radiating from every nook and corner of the world.

"Adventures," remarked the talented Mr. Disraeli, "are for the adventurous," and it is to those who think of life as the supreme adventure that the Atlantic is most confidently addressed.

If you care for a magazine that satisfies, vexes and delights by turn, you can safely subscribe to the Atlantic Monthly for the coming year.

Public Service Railway Company, Newark, N. J. Amazonius 10, 1920. — To our Patrons : As a fair minded citizen, your impartial consideration of the facts set forth in subjoined letter, written by me to the Board of Public Utility Commissioners under date of Amazonius 7th. 1920, is respectfully requested. Very truly yours, Thomas N. McCarter, President.

To the Board of Public Utility Commissioners of the State of New Jersey, Trenton, New Jersey. Dear Sirs : The rate of fare of 7 cents, with one cent for a transfer, etc..., etc... Such large cities as Boston, New Haven, Hartford and Pittsburg already have a 10c. flat rate. Etc... etc... Under the foregoing statement of facts the company is forced to file herewith a flat rate of 10c. where 7c. is now charged. Etc... Etc...

> Now when Christmas bells ring clear
> Telling us that love is here
> And children sing
> Gifts that speak of thoughtful love
> Just like angels from above
> Glad tidings bring.

Rugs, mirrors, chairs, tables, W. & J. Sloane, N.Y., Wash., San F. Christmas Gifts Sure to be Appreciated. : Standing lamps, table lamps, book ends, Sheffield ware, desk sets, framed prints, porcelains, soft pillows, foot rests (D-2968 Rocking foot rest in Mahogany. Formerly $45.00. Sale Price $30.00!) sconces, mantel clocks, wall clocks, tall clocks, small tables, smoking stands, occasional chairs, screens, oriental rugs, Chinese embroideries, vacuum cleaners — Mirrors. Small Oriental Rugs : Mossouls, Pergames, Beloochistans, Lilehennas, Sarouks and Kirmanshahs.

California was peopled by the Indians first and then by the Padres who brought with them their sprigs of vine and of orange and of fig and also the art of irrigation. So that you will find today from the very northermost part, from Klamath Lake down to the Imperial Valley in the South, the lands of California watered and made as fertile as the valley of the Nile.

That's all right. Yes Sir. But I come from the Eastern shore of Maryland. I'm an East Sho' man. Have you ever been on the Eastern Sho'? No? Well sir, we're a strange people and we have some strange legends on the East Sho'. When Adam and Eve lived in the Garden of Eden they fell sick and the Lord was very much disturbed over them, so he called a council of his angels and wanted to know where they should be taken for a change of air.

Gabriel suggested the Eastern Sho' of Maryland but the Lord said, No, No ; that wouldn't be sufficient change.

Yes sir, down at Chincoteague they have the biggest and the finest oysters in the world. Big as your hand and when you get a half dozen of them a couple of hours out of the water you know you have something.

It was at Chincoteague two Spanish galleons went ashore in the old days and some ponies swam ashore. To this day they have a yearly round-up on the island where the breed of these ponies is coralled, a short special breed of horse.

Tangier Island is another place. That's where the sheriff shot the boy who wouldn't go in off his front porch on Sunday morning during church service. Either in church or in the house during that hour. He shot him all right. They have little individual canals up to their back doors from the bay.

And the native, coming up to him suddenly with a knife as long as your arm, said, *Yo soy mas hombre que tu*! and started a swing at him. Had he not been so quick to seize a chair and bring it down on the man's head — What would have happened?

CHAPTER XIX

OMETIMES the men would come in and say there was a turkey nest down in the meadow and they'd send me to look for it.

Once I fell in the mireage up to my waist. My, they was mad at me. "Can't tramp a meadow without falling in the mireage?" they said.

I miss it often. At nine they let me drive the hay-hoist with one horse and later with two. One morning I had the young team out. It was Allie's team of greys, they was only just no more than colts. They shied at a piece of paper. I could hear the men up in the barn yelling. "Hey, what's the matter down there!" But it was no use. I tried to get to their heads. I wasn't afraid of them. Allie said afterward he wouldn't have been surprised to have seen me killed.

One of the women stood in the road waving a broom. I can see her yet. I might have been able to manage them if it hadn't been for her but they simply jumped over a wagon and smashed the hay-fork and ran down the road two miles. Then they came back again. My but the old man was mad at me. All the black looks I got!

I used to hate the Old Man. Sometimes I'd be getting wood and he'd ask me why I hadn't done something. I'd say I hadn't gotten round to it yet. Maybe he'd throw a piece of wood at me.

I can remember the churning. I wouldn't exactly like to go back to it all but sometimes I miss it terribly. Sometimes it would n't take you more than five minutes to get the butter and sometimes you'd churn for 45 or two hours and sometimes it would never come. We'd get four or five pounds or more at a churning. Then it would have to be washed and salted and packed in jars in the cellar.

So now that it is raining. So now that it is Amazonius — we go to buy a metal syringe at the factory because we know the men who live on our street who own the bricks that make the walls that hold the floors that hold the girls who make mistakes in the inventories :

Every order that comes in is copied. You must rely on your help. As the orders come in they are handled by a girl who puts them on our own uniform order sheets. So right there it begins. You have to rely on a young flyaway who has perhaps been up dancing the night before. It's easy enough for her to write "with" for "without" and — that's the sort of thing that happens. There is a certain minimum of error that you must count on and no reputable house will fail to make good promptly.

The glass blowers have never in my entire experience of 17 years suffered any harm from their trade. Why we had a boy in the old factory, a cripple, a withered leg, the weakest, scrawniest lad you ever saw. He's been blowing for us for 15 or 17 years and you should see him today. Why the fat fairly hangs down over his collar.

In our thermometer work they blow the bulb then fill it with mercury which is in a special container like the cups you get at Child's restaurant say. They never have to touch the stuff. When the bulb is full they seal it. Then the mercury in the bulb is warmed by passing the bulb through a flame. This is to drive it up the capillary tube. There can be no volatilization since the mercury is in the tube and this is the only time the stuff is heated. Then when the metal rises from the heat the other end of the glass is dipped in the stuff so that as the bulb now cools the mercury is sucked up filling the thermometer completely.

Sometimes, of course, a bulb breaks in heating so that the floor is full of the stuff.

The hydrofluoric acid for marking is used under a hood with a special exhaust-blower that has nothing else to do but exhaust that hood. There is not the slightest odor of fumes in the room. The air is as good there as here.

And what is your business?

Rag merchant.

Ah yes. And what does that mean?

Our main specialty is shoddy.

Ah yes. Shoddy is made from —

[77]

From woolen rags. The whole mass is put into a vat and the cotton dissolved out. It comes out in a great wet heap of stuff that has to be washed and dried.

Sometimes they burn the cotton out with gas. For instance you'll see a piece of cloth, grey cloth. The gas will take out the black cotton and leave the wool fibres all running in one direction. One of the secrets of the trade is the selection of the colors. That is red shoddy is made from red rags and so on. But they even take the dyes out of the cloth and use it over again.

You know the army coats the boys wore. They were 70 % shoddy. It's all wool but the fibre has been broken. It makes a hard material not like the soft new woven woolens but it's wool, all of it.

After the stuff from the vats is dry they put it on the donkeys which turn it into loose skeins. From that stage it goes on to the making of the yarn for weaving when any quantity of fresh wool can be mixed that you desire.

The shortest fibre, that can't be used for anything else, is made into these workingmen's shirts you see. The wool is held in a container in the loosest state possible. This is connected up with a blower in front of which a loom is set for weaving a fairly tight cotton mesh. Then as the loom is working the wool is BLOWN IN! Where the cotton warp and woof cross the shoddy is caught.

Recently a Jew came in to complain of the lightness of the shirts he was getting. All we did was to yell out, "George turn on the blower a little stronger." One washing and the wool is gone. But the Jews are the smart ones. You got to hand it to them. They invent machinery to do anything with that stuff. Why one man made a million before the government stopped him by making cheap quilts.

He took any kind of rags just as they were collected, filth or grease right on them the way they were and teased them up into a fluffy stuff which he put through a rolling process and made into sheets of wadding. These sheets were fed mechanically between two layers of silkolene and a girl simply sat there with an electric sewing device which she guided with her hand and drew in the designs you see on those quilts, you know.

You've seen this fake oilcloth they are advertising now.

Congoleum. Nothing but building paper with a coating of enamel.

¡O vida tan dulce!